LOVE
COME HOME

LOVE
COME HOME

ROBERT H. PIERSON

REVIEW AND HERALD PUBLISHING ASSOCIATION
Washington, DC 20039-0555
Hagerstown, MD 21740

Copyright © 1987 by
Review and Herald Publishing Association

This book was
Edited by Gerald Wheeler
Designed by Richard Steadham
Cover photos by Meylan Thoresen
Type set: 11/12 Zapf

Printed in U.S.A.

Library of Congress Cataloging in Publication Data

Pierson, Robert H.
    Love come home.

    1. God—Love—Biblical teaching. 2. God—Worship
and love—Biblical teaching. 3. Bible. O.T. Hosea—
Meditations. 4. Bible. N.T. Philemon—Meditations.
5. Seventh-day Adventists. 6. Adventists. I. Title.
BS544.P54 1988   242'.5   87-9675

ISBN 0-8280-0391-2

Contents

Foreword

Love Come Home is a series of meditations on the Bible books of Hosea and Philemon. Uppermost in the author's mind has been the desire to present material that will challenge the reader spiritually, applying lessons from ancient Israel and the early church to the Seventh-day Adventist Church today—especially as they affect the individual church member. Some chapters will use the biblical books as a springboard for related issues. In chapter 4 (on happy marriages) and chapter 2 (on hazards to a happy marriage) my presentations wander a bit from the Hosea and Gomer drama in order to zero in on practical lessons for Seventh-day Adventist homes in our day.

This book not only seeks to challenge every reader to a better appreciation of Hosea and Philemon, but also to appeal for a new personal commitment to the Lord Jesus Christ and His last-day message, and to make some little contribution to the creation of happier Seventh-day Adventist homes.

—Robert H. Pierson

The Winds of Change Blow

It was a moment I shall never forget.

Arms flailing, Dr. Rob Newbold came galloping down the hill to meet Elder Leonard Robinson and me as we drove onto the Ngoma Mission Hospital grounds in Rwanda. "It's terrible," he screamed. "They're burning our villages and killing our people. We're sure glad you're here!" His words tumbled out as he described the events of the past few days. "Look out over the mountains. What do you see?"

I did—and saw smoke spiraling heavenward from several burning villages. A few hundred yards away several hundred agitated tribesmen who had fled for refuge to the mission compound now huddled together in groups discussing their sad plight.

The frightening fifties and the smoking sixties were years of dislocation and violence in the many newly independent states of Africa. The continent was awash with violent change. Many countries erupted into existence—some of them unprepared for the responsibilities of nationhood so suddenly thrust upon them. I know. I served in those countries in turmoil for many of those years. Too often I was right in the midst of the shouting and the shooting. Often I visited African Adventists in detention camps. By the hour I listened to their plaintive accounts of violence, arson, theft, murder, and persecution. Harold Macmillan, prime minister of Great Britain at the time, described what was happening in Africa as "a wind of change" sweeping over the continent. It was a time of terror and trial for hundreds of thousands of hapless African tribesmen as they sought to adjust and cope with the new way of life.

Another Era of Change

Some 26 centuries before the flames of violence roared through much of Africa, winds of change ravaged other parts of the world. The eighth and the seventh centuries B.C. were periods of radical transformation in Europe and in the Bible lands of the Middle East. E. H. Robertson calls those years the turning point of ancient history—a period when "all the world seems astir" (in J. B. Phillips, *Four Prophets* [New York: Macmillan Co., 1963], pp. xxiii, xxiv).

Rome, the so-called eternal city, was little more than a village, while Celtic refugees poured into Cornwall. Greece had not yet reached the glory of fifth-century Athens, though Homer was already writing and had fashioned the language and literary models for the later dramatists. Pericles had not yet built the Parthenon, but the skills he needed and even the artistic forms arose in that century. It was a time of Assyrian might and Egyptian culture.

"Over the whole world the Spirit of God stirred the spirit of man. In Judah and Israel four men spoke in the name of the living God, conscious of why they spoke. They knew nothing of the world movement but they were at the heart of it" (*ibid.*, p. xxv).

"A characteristic of this century everywhere was that it prepared the way for great events" (*ibid.*). "After this century, history took a new turn and we live in the aftermath and results of their words, spoken at the dawn of an age that was to include the coming of Jesus Christ and all the great religions as we know them" *(ibid.,* p. xxvii).

The eighth century before the birth of Christ was a period of crisis for the northern kingdom of Israel. The dark cloud of apostasy settled upon it. The people had forgotten God and His moral precepts. A time of inhumanity toward fellow men, it ground the depressed poor further into the dust of abject poverty. Wealth, power, selfish accomplishment, and pleasure became the false gods substituted for the One who had led them out of Egyptian bondage.

Dishonesty, suppression, greed, and moral depravity left little room for the needs and the feelings of the less fortunate. The Inspired Word faithfully chronicles the depravity of the human heart in the days of Israel: "Hear the word of the Lord, ye children of Israel: for the Lord hath a controversy with the inhabitants of the land, because there is no truth, nor mercy, nor knowledge of God in the land. By swearing, and lying, and killing, and stealing, and committing adultery, they break out, and blood toucheth blood" (Hosea 4:1, 2).

If the moral condition of Israel during those dark centuries was bleak indeed, the political outlook for the nation's very survival was, as well, dismal. Enemy states on its borders threatened to become the agents of God's wrath and national ruin. Throughout their history, the Israelites had depended upon the mercy and the goodness of their God to protect and to deliver them from aggressor nations bent upon their destruction. Now He would withdraw that protection.

In His love and mercy God seeks to intervene and arrest Israel and the southern kingdom of Judah in their headstrong rush to destruction. His unchanging, compassionate love permeates the inspired accounts of this period of Israel's apostasy. Listen to the appeals of His prophets: "O Israel, thou hast destroyed thyself; but in me is thine help. I will be thy king: where is any other that may save thee in all thy cities? and thy judges of whom thou saidst, Give me a king and princes?" (Hosea 13:9, 10).

Foremost among His messengers during this crucial period were Amos, Hosea, Isaiah, and Micah. Such "holy men of God spake as they were moved by the Holy Ghost" (2 Peter 1:21).

Prophets are individuals whom the Almighty selected to make known His will to His people. "And he said, Hear now my words: If there be a prophet among you, I the Lord will make myself known unto him in a vision, and will speak unto him in a dream" (Num. 12:6).

In response to such communications from the Holy Spirit Amos declared, "Thus saith the Lord" (Amos 1:3, 6, 9, etc.). Of similar communications to Hosea the Scriptures record, "The word of the Lord that came unto Hosea," "and the Lord said unto him" (Hosea 1:1, 4). In his prophecy against Syria and Israel, Isaiah wrote, "Moreover the Lord said unto me" (Isa. 8:1). When Isaiah spoke God's truth to Hezekiah, the prophet testified to the divine source of his message: "Thus saith the Lord" (Isa. 38:1). The prophet Micah confirmed that the source of his messages: "The word of the Lord that came to Micah" and "hear ye now what the Lord saith" (Micah 1:1; 6:1). Such clear statements should leave no doubt as to the divine origin of God's messages to His prophets.

Hosea

From among the prominent prophets of the eighth century before the birth of Christ, we shall devote our time and attention to Hosea—the author of the Old Testament book bearing his name. Our sources for his life and labors are scarce indeed. What we know from inspired sources about the prophet is what we mine from his book and from the writings of Ellen White.

That Hosea was a native of the northern kingdom seems certain. He is familiar with many places in Israel and mentions them in his writings. Referring to Samaria frequently, he writes of cities, places, and persons identified with the northern kingdom.

Hosea's affinity for, or his identity with, the life of the farmer seems apparent through his allusions to heifers, lambs, calves, horses, fowls, grapes, fig trees, roots and fruit, empty vines, grain ("corn," KJV), flocks and herds, the winepress, the plow and clods, sowing and reaping, plowing, breaking up the fallow ground, furrows of the field, and other terms normally associated with farming.

His marriage to Gomer, which brought years of heartbreak and estrangement, finally ended in her leaving home and becoming even more involved in immoral relationships. Many scholars believe that she might have been a cult prostitute, one who participated in the fertility rites of Baal worship.

God uses the painful story of Hosea's blighted romance and marriage, marred as it was by Gomer's unfaithfulness to her husband and to God Himself, to depict His people's spiritual adultery. Hosea's love and fidelity to his wanton wife reveal the nature of a compassionate God appealing to wandering Israel to return to Him in repentance and lasting commitment.

His Message

The withering indictments of Israel's sinful course contained in Hosea's prophecies are foreboding ones indeed. They sharply rebuke the nation's persistent sin. Yet they also contain assurances of unfailing love and poignant appeals for Israel to repent and return to God.

With his contemporaries, Amos, Isaiah, and Micah, Hosea sought courageously to stem the tide of apostasy in the kingdoms of Judah and Israel. Their scathing denunciations of sin in the camp leave no room for anyone to question whether they faithfully discharged their prophetic office.

Hosea also relayed God's tender appeals for loyalty, seeking to arouse some smoldering embers of the love the chosen people of God had once known. Over and over he painted the picture of the Lord as Israel's true Lover, One who patiently waits and longs for some sign of recognition on the part of His straying people. God is the loving, compassionate Father yearning over a wayward child. He is the disappointed husband, willing to forgive and forget the unfaithfulness of His adulterous wife.

Looking down through the millennia, Hosea sees a time when God's people will respond to the entreaties of her Divine Lover. It is certain to come—though God has had to delay the end time as He awaits a people who keep the commandments of God and glory in the faith of Jesus as they prepare for their marriage to the heavenly Bridegroom.

Hosea proclaims a very practical, present-worldly message. He does not deal with illusive philosophy and theology that might escape the understanding of those he seeks to awaken. With almost terrifying precision, he points an accusing finger at all of Israel. With the terrifying tones of one who is certain of the Source from which his message comes, he declares, as did Nathan, "Thou art the man."

The prophet was not a preacher courting the favor and the plaudits of his "congregation." Nor was he concerned that his straight testimony might be his professional undoing and cause his church board to recommend to the conference committee that it defrock him or send him elsewhere. Conciliation for commendation, compromise in exchange for approval, soft-pedaling or soft-soaping—such things had no place in Hosea's pastoral tool kit.

The prophet spared no words, evaded no opportunity, to proclaim the plain, unadulterated truth of God. He presented God's message and trusted Him to accomplish its intended purpose.

It is human to seek to avoid responsibility for doing the distasteful and the difficult. At times God's truth can be unpalatable, His Word uncomfortable. The sinner may squirm uneasily or may retaliate in anger. But Hosea knew, as true servants of God have always known, that he must carry to others God's straight message, whatever the cost.

Where the Shadows Are Never Lifted

"The Lord said to Hosea, Go, take unto thee a wife" (Hosea 1:2).

Marriage at best is somewhat of a gamble. In too many unions one or both parties lose. A broken home in turn often devastates many other lives.

The greatest decision any person ever makes is to choose Jesus Christ as his personal Saviour. The second most important one is to select a life's companion. Happiness or misery, heaven or hell, frequently hang in the balance. "Marriage is something that will influence and affect your life both in this world and in the world to come" (*The Adventist Home*, p. 43).

"If those who are contemplating marriage would not have miserable, unhappy reflections after marriage, they must make it a subject of serious, earnest reflection now. This step taken unwisely is one of the most effective means of ruining the usefulness of young men and women. Life becomes a burden, a curse" (*ibid.*).

An old adage reads "Marry in haste, repent at leisure." Today many translate it, "If at first you don't succeed, try, try again." Instead, every committed Christian should have as his or her motto, "Look very,

very carefully before you leap." Some wise man has suggested that "love is blind." He should have added, "It is also deaf." Young men and women with plans for marriage are in little mood to listen to advice.

If you don't believe it, listen to this story:

Henry was a fine, upstanding young man. After a rocky teenage experience, he settled down as a solid citizen in the community and an active member in the church. In fact, some of the church leaders were considering him for church office.

Then boy met girl. In this case, Henry met Blossom. When he "fell," he did so hard. Blossom was a pretty girl. She dressed nicely and always seemed to have boys around her. Sure that she was the girl for him, Henry started getting serious.

His father was not so sure. "Take it easy, son," he cautioned. "You can't always tell what is behind a pretty face."

"That's right," an older sister agreed. "Blossom doesn't rate too high with the other girls I know. Usually, girls know each other pretty well."

Some of the church members also cautioned him. Several spoke to him about his plans for the future.

Ellen White came into the picture at this juncture. "You have steadily refused to be cautioned by your father, your loving sister, or by your friends in the church," she wrote him. "I came to you as Christ's ambassador; but your strong feelings, your self-confidence, closed your eyes to danger and your ears to warnings. Your course has been as persistent as though no one knew quite so much as yourself or as though the salvation of your soul depended upon your following your own judgment" (*Testimonies*, vol. 5, p. 106).

Whether the young man heeded her, we do not know. If the law of averages held good—he did not. And if the law of averages continued after the wedding, he probably wished many times he had listened.

In an effort to help safeguard the happiness and the permanence of marriage on the part of Seventh-day Adventists, the North American Division Committee on Administration in the 1968 Annual Council adopted the following action:

"The Spirit of Prophecy established guidelines for men and women contemplating marriage, pointing out the inadvisability of marriage where:

1. "There is a great disparity in age."
2. "There is poor health in either party."
3. "There is financial irresponsibility."
4. "There are differences in ethnic and cultural backgrounds that are irreconcilable."
5. "There are different racial backgrounds."

"In dealing with a couple seriously contemplating marriage, where both parties are members of the Seventh-day Adventist Church, it becomes the duty of the minister to call attention to this counsel, pointing out the dangers involved before uniting such in marriage, recognizing, however, that none of these aspects as such constitutes a moral issue."

The action now appears in the *Manual for Ministers*, p. 120.

Ellen White adds the following helpful and far-reaching words on preparation for marriage: "Those who are contemplating marriage should consider what will be the character and influence of the home they are founding. As they become parents, a sacred trust is committed to them. Upon them depends in a great measure the well-being of their children in this world, and their happiness in the world to come. To a great extent they determine both the physical and the moral stamp that the little ones receive. And upon the character of the home depends the condition of society; the weight of each family's influence will tell in the upward or the downward scale" *(The Adventist Home,* p. 44).

"Weigh every sentiment, and watch every development of character in the one with whom you think to link your life destiny. The step you are about to take is one of the most important in your life, and should not be taken hastily. While you may love, do not love blindly" *(ibid.,* p. 45).

It is well for the bride and groom to remember that the vows they repeat on the wedding day are not only to each other—they are entering upon a covenant with God as well. Then they will honestly endeavor, to the best of their ability and with the help of God, to keep those vows as long as they shall live. A wedding is not only a legal contract; it is, indeed, a covenant witnessed in heaven. God records the promises made there.

"Everywhere you go, Elder Pierson, tell the young people to heed well the counsel the Bible and the Spirit of Prophecy give on marrying unbelievers." The speaker was a late-middle-aged woman attending camp meeting in one of our North American conferences. "I thought I would be able to convert my fiancé and that he would join the church after we had been married a little while."

She paused, then continued sorrowfully, "But it hasn't worked out that way. Our home has not been a happy one. Sister White was right when she spoke of homes 'where the shadows are never lifted.' I've had one like that for more than 30 years. I've scarcely known a day of happiness in my married life."

The apostle Paul wrote the same thing centuries ago: "Do not unite yourselves with unbelievers; they are no fit mates for you. What has righteousness to do with wickedness? Can light consort with darkness? Can Christ agree with Belial, or a believer join hands with an unbeliever?" (2 Cor. 6:14, 15, NEB).

"No one who fears God can without danger connect himself with one who fears Him not. 'Can two walk together, except they be agreed?' The happiness and prosperity of the marriage relation depends upon the unity of the parties; but between the believer and the unbeliever there is a radical difference of tastes, inclinations, and purposes. They are serving two masters, between whom there can be no concord. However pure and correct one's principles may be, the influence of an unbelieving companion will have a tendency to lead away from God" (*Messages to Young People*, p. 464).

How many young men and women have, too late and to their bitter regret, discovered the truthfulness of Mrs. White's words.

The greatest hazard or danger to a happy home is failure to accord God His rightful place in the family. The climate of love can thrive in the family only when the God of love is present to mold the thinking and the actions of family members.

When the family altar falls into disrepair, or the members neglect it entirely, we witness the first step taken in crowding God out of the home. This is a real danger and threat today. Both father and mother hold down jobs to keep the family viable. Children live under the pressure of school and peer activity. Life is a daily mad rush. Some things get crowded out. Often it is easy for family worship to be the loser in the battle for time.

Ellen White reminds us to make the family worship period happy, rewarding, and relevant for every member of the family. She tells us to see that it is "pleasant and interesting" (*Testimonies*, vol. 5, p. 335), the "most pleasant and enjoyable [time] of the day" (*ibid.*, vol. 7, p. 43). If we make family worship "brief and full of life" (*Education*, p. 186), it will not be forgotten so easily.

Keep God in your family life. When He is there, love, happiness, peace, and contentment will reign. We crowd Him out to our peril. "Seek ye first the kingdom of God, and his righteousness; and all these things [true happiness] shall be added unto you" (Matt. 6:33).

Money Can Threaten Marital Happiness

Bill was quite young when he married Lisa. In fact, too young. He was also just entering college. Working at odd jobs while taking classwork did not provide many of life's luxuries. Then problems arose because Lisa wanted *things*. It took money to acquire them. When the budget was tight, she was resentful. Money became a point of contention as Bill resented her insensitive demands. More and more he controlled the purse strings, which nettled her. Love fled the scene as hurt and resentment filled the home. Eventually they came to a parting of the ways. Once again money had created another marital statistic.

If a couple are to have a happy home, they must have a clear understanding about finances. Who controls it? What is it to be spent for? "Here are things which should be considered," Ellen White writes. "Is [she] an economist, or will she, if married, not only use all her own earnings, but all of yours to gratify a vanity?" (The Adventist Home, p. 46).

"The love of money is the first step toward all kinds of sin. Some people have even turned away from God because of their love for it, and as a result have pierced themselves with many sorrows" (1 Tim. 6:10, TLB).

Do You Communicate?

"Experts claim that one of the most serious problems in marriage and a prime cause of divorce lies in the inability or reluctance of couples to communicate" (Nancy Van Pelt, How to Communicate With Your Mate, p. 3). Dr. Daniel Sugarman, a practicing psychotherapist, declares, "I have never seen a troubled marriage in which communication was not a problem." He then explains, "When the fragile lines of communication between a husband and a wife become disconnected, important messages can no longer be sent or received" (Reader's Digest, September 1976, p. 92).

"I married a sphinx," a woman once wrote. "All my husband ever does is grunt—he never talks with me."

Should an Engagement Ever Be Broken?

My young friend was heartbroken. The girl of his dreams had just "stood him up." They had set the wedding date and mailed the invitations. Now this!

"How could she do it?" Jim sobbed. "All our plans were made. We were so happy—at least I thought we were. Now she tells me she can't go through with it. She isn't sure!"

My words of human comfort must have sounded rather empty. "You know, Jim, someday it may look different to you. It is much better to find out now that she really didn't love you than to discover it sometime after the wedding. Now the Lord can help you find someone else who will bring lasting happiness to you. What a tragedy it would have been for you both to be condemned to a life of unhappiness and probable divorce!"

Are there ever any circumstances under which you should terminate an engagement? Listen to what Ellen White declares: "You may say, 'But I have given my promise, and shall I now retract it?' I answer, If you have made a promise contrary to the Scriptures, by all means retract it without delay, and in humility before God repent of the infatuation that led you to make so rash a pledge. Far better take back such a promise, in the fear of God, than keep it, and thereby dishonor your Maker" *(The Adventist Home*, pp. 48, 49).

Better a few days of heartbreak now than a lifetime of wretched regret later!

I Will Bind You to Me Forever

Hosea 2:19, TLB

Tiny Tyler Smith was aglow. Never in all of his 6 years had the little orphan known the luxury of clean white sheets, nourishing food, and such attention as he was now receiving. It seemed worth being sick to spend a few days in the hospital.

As the white uniformed nurse paused to tuck Tyler in for the night, the little fellow looked up into her face and said timidly, "I *like* you!"

"I love you," the vision in white replied.

"What is love?" the little urchin asked.

Leaning over, the nurse took him in her arms and for a few breathtaking moments, held him close to her.

The boy stared, wide-eyed, from his bed and gasped enthusiastically, "I like love!"

Almost everyone likes love. One has but to observe the tender scenes on beaches and in parks when signs of spring appear to confirm this observation.

I Will Court Her Again

Hosea and Gomer liked love too—at first—for a while. When Gomer drifted deeper into her unfaithfulness, Hosea patiently sought to win her back. "I will allure her" (Hosea 2:14), or "I will court her again," as *The Living Bible* records his reaction. The time will come, the prophet assured himself, when "she will call me 'My Husband' instead of 'My Master' " (verse 16, TLB).

His love and faith endured all of the cruel pangs of a cheated husband, yet he continued his efforts to win back her affection. Some day "she will respond to me there, singing with joy as in days long ago in her youth" (verse 15, TLB).

His love knew no limits. The long agonizing nights alone. The children that were probably not his born into the home. The months or years Gomer may have spent as a prostitute in the streets or places of Baal worship. Even when Gomer stood on the auction block of the slave market, naked, used, and discarded by one lustful lover after another, he was the husband who still loved her (Hosea 3:1-3).

His undying affection for his wanton wife was a living, gripping lesson to a backsliding, apostate Israel. Through the prophet and his love, God longed to impress upon His people His great love for them despite their disloyalty and sin.

God's Love for Wayward Israel

God's repeated assurance of love for Israel fills the book of Hosea. "I will betroth thee unto me for ever," he declares (verse 19). Though God let adversity and suffering come to Israel in an endeavor to win back their allegiance, He still loved its people. "He hath torn, and he will heal us," the prophet declares; "he hath smitten, and he will bind us up" (Hosea 6:1).

"O Ephraim, what shall I do unto thee?" God asks in agony of love (verse 4). Then, in an effort to explain both His concern and compassion, Hosea speaks for Him, "I desired mercy, and not sacrifice; and knowledge of God more than burnt offerings" (verse 6). "I want your love; . . . I want you to know me" (TLB).

In a plaintive appeal, God agonizes, "How shall I give thee up, Ephraim? how shall I deliver thee, Israel? how shall I make thee as Admah? how shall I set thee as Zeboim? mine heart is turned within me, my repentings are kindled together" (Hosea 11:8). "I led Israel with my ropes of love. . . . I myself have stooped and fed him," the Lord reminisces (verse 4, TLB) "I took care of you in the wilderness, in that dry and thirsty land" (Hosea 13:5, TLB).

"I am the Lord thy God, . . ." Jehovah reminds Israel, "and thou shalt know no god but me: for there is no saviour beside me" (verse 4). "I am living and strong! I look after you and care for you. . . . My mercies never fail" (Hosea 14:8, TLB). "My love will know no bounds" (verse 4, TLB).

Then, as though making one last agonized appeal, the prophet cries, "Therefore turn thou to thy God: keep mercy and judgment and wait on thy God continually" (Hosea 12:6).

His Love Is Beyond Compare

The love of God for ancient Israel was but a demonstration of His love and compassion for His people throughout all time. "I have loved thee with an everlasting love" (Jer. 31:3).

God's love is "amazing" (*Steps to Christ*, p. 22). It is "boundless" (*Testimonies*, vol. 7, p. 225); "everlasting" (*Child Guidance*, pp. 26, 27); "infinite" and "exhaustless" (*Testimonies*, vol. 5, p. 740); "great and . . . unfailing" (*The Ministry of Healing*, p. 229); "unfathomable" (*Gospel Workers*, p. 51); "matchless" (*Testimonies*, vol. 4, p. 146). His great love for us is, indeed, beyond human expression.

"The dominant theme of the book of Hosea is the love of God for His erring children. The experiences through which the prophet passed in his own family life, and the feelings of his own heart toward his faithless wife, gave him a glimpse into the boundless depths of the Father's love for His people" *(The SDA Bible Commentary*, vol. 4, p. 886).

Ellen White reminds us that God loves the whole church—His people in Hosea's day, His people in ours. It has members who are imperfect, unlovable, weak, discouraged, even backslidden. Yet many, thank God, are saints in the truest sense of the word. God loves those in single-parent homes and those who choose life alone, as well as those in homes with many children. He loves them all!

God's Love Embraces the Whole World

Human love is often narrow. God's love is all-inclusive. It embraces a whole world in sin, a whole church—the weak and the strong. No one can ever accuse God of not loving him.

God loves the Eastern church as well as the Western. He loves the black, the white, the brown, the red, the yellow. The Lord has no favorites, knows nothing of a superrace. "He caused to spring from one forefather people of every race" (Acts 17:26, Weymouth). "There is no preferential treatment with God" (Rom. 2:11, Phillips).

"We are all supposed to be preparing for the same heaven. We have the same heavenly Father, the same Redeemer, who loved us and gave Himself for us all, without any distinction" (E. G. White to Elder Hyatt, in South Africa, Feb. 15, 1900).

God Loves the Weak Ones

God loves the weak ones in the church. Aren't you thankful for this assurance? Many of us fall in this category. We love the Lord and desire to serve Him, but we are quite weak. Frequently we stumble and fall. The precious promise to such is: "While we were still helpless" (Rom. 5:6, Weymouth). "The . . . weak are bound by a chain of sympathy closely to His heart" (*Testimonies to Ministers*, p. 19). During Christ's earthly ministry He seized every opportunity to help them. Stooping down, He lifted them up and spoke words of encouragement that enabled them to persevere despite life's problems and reverses.

God Loves the Tempted Ones

God loves the tempted ones in His church—and that includes all of us—in Hosea's day and in our own. We can praise God that we have help when the evil one comes with his searing temptations. "There hath no temptation taken you but such as is common to man: but God is faithful, who will not suffer you to be tempted above that ye are able; but will with the temptation also make a way of escape, that ye may be able to bear it" (1 Cor. 10:13).

"Feeling the terrible power and temptation, . . . many a man cries in despair, 'I cannot resist evil.' Tell him that he can, that he must resist. He may have been overcome again and again, but it need not be always thus. He is weak in moral power, controlled by the habits of a life of sin. His promises and resolutions are like ropes of sand. The knowledge of his broken promises and forfeited pledges weakens his confidence in his own sincerity, and causes him to feel that

God cannot accept him. . . . But he need not despair" *(The Ministry of Healing,* pp. 174, 175).

God Loves the Discouraged Ones

God loves the discouraged members among His people. Much in the world today will bring discouragement if we permit it. Ill health. Death of loved ones. Financial reverses. Poverty. The cares of life press down many. Others find themselves depressed by the lack of love on the part of fellow church members—or by affairs within their family circle. Some are almost ready to give up.

To such the voice of courage comes, "The Lord God of thy fathers hath said unto thee; fear not, neither be discouraged" (Deut. 1:21). "When thou passest through the waters, I will be with thee; and through the rivers, they shall not overflow thee: when thou walkest through the fire, thou shalt not be burned; neither shall the flame kindle upon thee" (Isa. 43:2).

The next time you feel discouragement stealing over you, remember: "To all who are reaching out to feel the guiding hand of God, the moment of greatest discouragement is the time when divine help is nearest. They will look back with thankfulness upon the darkest part of their way. 'The Lord knoweth how to deliver the godly' (2 Peter 2:9). From every temptation and every trial He will bring them forth with firmer faith and a richer experience" *(The Desire of Ages,* p. 528).

"God would send every angel in heaven to the aid of such a one, rather than allow him to be overcome" *(Testimonies,* vol. 7, p. 17).

God Loves the Backsliders

God loves the backsliders in the church—those who

feel unloved, unwanted. Those wounded by unkind words and thoughtless actions. Those who don't come to church anymore—but many of whom still love the Lord and believe His last-day message.

Paul describes the backslider as one who was "spiritually dead through your sins and failures, all the time that you followed this world's ideas of living, and obeyed the evil ruler of the spiritual realm" (Eph. 2:1, 2, Phillips).

Of such God said in Hosea's day, "I drew them with . . . bands of love. . . . How shall I give thee up? (Hosea 11:4-8).

I shall never forget a young couple attending a South African camp meeting. During the testimony period of the early-morning service the husband said, "My wife has been praying for me for 13 years. I have been a backslider for many years. I want to come back to God this morning. I want her to stand with me so we can dedicate our lives to God and to His service together."

That precious scene I have witnessed numberless times in many lands. Men and women—backsliders whom the Lord loves with an everlasting love—coming back to Him! Those "bands of love" have pulled them back to the family of God.

Jesus describes the joy God feels when even one who has strayed from God's love and way returns home. "I say unto you, that likewise joy shall be in heaven over one sinner that repenteth, more than over ninety and nine just persons, which need no repentance" (Luke 15:7).

God Loves His Saints

Most of all, God loves the saints in His church—the

large numbers who love Him supremely and who, every day, seek to be sure that they walk in harmony with His will. I've met thousands of them around the world. Brown saints. Yellow saints. Black saints. White saints. Red saints. God loves us all!

If He loves the sinner who hates or ignores Him, if He gave His life for those who have no time for Him, think how much He must love those who seek to serve Him faithfully!

"He that spared not his own Son, but delivered him up for us all, how shall he not with him also freely give us all things?" (Rom. 8:32).

"He did not spare his own Son, but gave him up for us all; and with this gift how can he fail to lavish upon us all he has to give?" (NEB).

Paul's words to the Roman Christians are a constant assurance for those of us who love and serve Him today—"The proof of God's amazing love is this: that it was while we were sinners that Christ died for us. Moreover, if he did that for us while we were sinners, now that we are men justified by the shedding of his blood, what reason have we to fear?" (Rom. 5:8, 9, Phillips).

God's people were the Gomers of Hosea's day. If we are of Laodicea today, perhaps we are the modern Gomers. Our bent for sinning makes us so. But God declares to His people of all times, "I will heal their backsliding, I will love them freely." "I drew them with cords of a man, with bands of love." "Thou art my people" (Hosea 14:4; 11:4; 2:23).

God's Unquenchable Love

How unquenchable was Hosea's love for Gomer? That love filled him with an eager longing to win her back—to bring her home again.

His love for his straying wife but faintly typified the mighty love of God for Israel in his day and for His lukewarm, blind, and naked church today (see Rev. 3:15-22). For you. For me. For that straying son or daughter, father or mother, brother or sister, friend or neighbor for whom you are praying. God loves them more than you possibly could. He is more concerned about their salvation than we could ever be!

In a burst of sublime assurance, the Lord's messenger describes God's love for His people in Hosea's day, in our day, and forever: "All the paternal love which has come down from generation to generation through the channel of human hearts, all the springs of tenderness which have opened in the souls of men, are but as a tiny rill to the boundless ocean when compared with the infinite, exhaustless love of God" (*Testimonies*, vol. 5, p. 740).

Ingredients of a Happy Marriage

September 2, 1981, was a very special day for Dollis and Robert Pierson. It was our *centennial*. Yes, I mean our *centennial*.

On that day we celebrated 50 years of happy married life and 50 years of preaching the everlasting gospel. Fifty plus 50 makes 100, doesn't it? So it *was* our centennial! In many ways ours might be described as a storybook romance—the football quarterback marries his high school sweetheart, and they live happily ever after—at least 57 years now.

Those 57 years have, indeed, been happy ones. Well over 50 percent of the credit for this beautiful experience goes to—you guessed it—my Dollis Mae! Forgetting Hosea and Gomer for a few minutes, I'm going to tell you a little about Dollis and the traits I appreciate about her. They have contributed substantially to our happy home. Perhaps sharing them will ignite a few fires of happiness in your home, whether you are a businessman, a minister, a church leader, a professional person, or whatever.

1. *Dollis takes an interest in my work.*

While I have been preaching, pastoring, counseling, chairing committees, Dollis has followed my work with attention. She was always doing what the ideal pastor's, or president's wife, can do best—taking an interest in the activities of the women—especially the wives of church employees. She also helped me with my extracurricular reading. I've developed many sermons and helped solve many problems as the result of her reading to me or sharing thoughts she has gleaned from her own reading.

2. *Dollis does not try to supervise me or my work.*

She did not try to "run" the church, the conference, the union, the division, or the General Conference. Her quiet interest and occasional suggestions helped. But never did she try to control or unduly influence my leadership.

Whether the following story is apocryphal, I do not know, but it seems that in one field the conference committeemen met in the living room of the president. Its members had struggled long to reach a consensus on one particular problem. The chairman was putting the proposed solution to a vote when a · feminine voice from the adjoining room said, "Be careful, Marvin. You had better counsel with the union about that before you vote it!"

Fortunately, I haven't had to live with a voice from the adjoining room.

3. *Dollis is careful what she says:* Being a president's wife for nearly 40 years has not always been easy. A wrong word, a slip, an inappropriate inflection in the wrong place by a leader's wife can create problems in a moment that take weeks—or years—to correct. Never, to my knowledge, has my wife embarrassed me publicly or privately by careless talk.

4. *Dollis tries to set a good example:* She dresses neatly and appropriately, avoiding extremes. Careful of her demeanor—gracious and friendly without affectation—she has many friends without making the mistake of cultivating special relationships with a favored few. Her church attendance—on the Sabbath

and at other meetings during the week—has always been exemplary. Her example before others has contributed to our home's happiness, for it has lessened the opportunities for criticism or tensions that usually affect both husband and wife.

5. *Dollis is thoughtful:* After living with her for 57 years, I can affirm that she treats me the same at home as she does in public. It is easy for family members to forget the words that oil the wheels of happiness in a home—"please," "thank you," and the other little magic phrases that help maintain a happy Christian atmosphere. She does not take me for granted.

6. *Dollis gives me time to be alone:* Some of us church leaders have had to live in a "goldfish bowl." We are always up front, usually in the middle of the action. It is difficult to get away after a meeting. Someone wants to speak with you "for just a minute." While such a program is rewarding and interesting, it is also extremely demanding and can drain a leader. Any husband who constantly has to deal with the public in his service to the church, to the company, to the boss, or to whomever faces the same type of problem.

I have been fortunate to have a companion who understands this and who provides time for me to be alone, to study, to pray, to think, to plan.

7. *Dollis prays with and for me:* Through the years of my ministry nothing has encouraged and sustained me in leadership more than the knowledge that many people were praying for me. Just before a General Conference session, an Annual Council, or some other important appointment, it was always a source of strength to receive letters from laypersons and church employees alike—some from faraway lands—saying,

"Elder Pierson, we are praying for you."

Dollis's prayers mean much to me. Before she goes with me for a speaking appointment, we always have prayer. While I am on the rostrum, whether before 20 or 20,000 persons, the knowledge that she is praying for me is an ever-present source of assurance.

8. *Dollis encourages me:* She is not one given to gushing flattery—not a bit of it. But in times of frustration or potential discouragement or when she knows much is at stake, she is always there. "It will work out all right." "The Lord will help you." "This too shall pass." "Don't worry about it; just trust the Lord!"

It has been that way for nearly 60 years. When I was playing football, basketball, or baseball in high school and our team was behind, or finding it tough going, encouragement from a special girl on the sidelines always renewed my determination and my will to win.

Perhaps I'm biased, but I happen to think that after 57 years of successful experience in that field, my Dollis Mae has something important to offer. In fact, I know she does.

I'm not naive enough to believe that I've brought forth any great new principles in husband/wife relationships here, but I also know that most of us need a bit of reminding now and again. We need to refresh our minds with principles that may have grown a bit dim—or fallen into disuse entirely.

Now, back to Hosea and Gomer.

A Lot of Loving

John and Marcia Thompson were looking for a child to adopt. In the orphanage they found themselves engulfed with many boys and girls, each of whom would gladly have become their child. Marcia wanted a little girl who would not only love them and fit into their family lifestyle but who also would be a help to her in the home.

Little carrot-topped Maria clung to her hand and cuddled up to her. "I'd like to be your little girl!" she lisped shyly.

"You would?" Mrs. Thompson queried. "And what can you do?"

The child looked up into her eyes pleadingly. "I can do a lot of loving," she replied.

"A lot of loving" is what makes family wheels run smoothly.

Hosea could "do a lot of loving." He had to, to put up with Gomer's trying ways. He might well have reasoned, "Let her go her own merry way! She isn't worth saving. She will never change!" But not Hosea— deep, abiding agape love inclines his heart toward wayward Gomer.

"I will court her again." "I will wait for you." "I will love [her] freely," he declared with faith-filled accents (Hosea 2:14; 3:2, TLB; 14:4).

Hosea cherished a love that will not let the other person go, no matter what treatment it may receive in turn. This kind of agape love never gives up.

When a scientist with his crystal prism passes a beam of white light through its refracting angles, the light comes out broken into beautiful component colors of the rainbow. Red. Blue. Yellow. Violet. Green. So love—the Christlike agape love—when passed through truly Christian hearts, minds, lips, hands, and feet, creates family love with all of its beautiful Christian graces.

The apostle Paul, in writing of this highest and best gift, describes the divine refraction experience in practical words. How laden with precious wisdom they should be to every Seventh-day Adventist home. Read them slowly. Read them thoughtfully. Read them prayerfully. More than that, read them with a desire and a determination in your heart to make them a living reality in your home:

"This love of which I speak is slow to lose patience—it looks for a way of being constructive. It is not possessive: it is neither anxious to impress nor does it cherish inflated ideas of its own importance.

"Love has good manners and does not pursue selfish advantage. It is not touchy. It does not keep account of evil or gloat over the wickedness of other people. . . . It shares the joy of those who live by the truth.

"Love knows no limit to its endurance, no end to its trust, no fading of its hope; it can outlast anything. Love never fails" (1 Cor. 13:4-8, Phillips).

Now read Paul's words again. And again. Love—true agape love—in your home or mine will make it what God intended homes should be. Love is, in fact, the one thing that will make Christian homes little heavens on earth. It is also the one thing that stands a chance of saving a troubled home when all else has failed.

Such love Hosea must have had. Such love—Jesus' love—is what you and I need. Like little carrot-top Maria, we will need to do "a lot of loving."

Don't Let Him Die!

"Don't let him die! He can't die now," the distraught voice on the other end of the line cried. "Oh, he can't die!"

"We will do our best," the hospital nurse assured

her. "He is getting the best possible care."

"I'll be there in half an hour. Please don't let him die!"

But Miriam arrived too late. Her father passed away before she could reach the hospital.

"Mother died three years ago," Miriam sobbed as she told the nurse the story. "Daddy and I had a terrible argument over my boyfriend several months later. My last words to him as I stormed out of the house were 'I hate you! I hate you!' But I didn't hate him. I loved him. He was a good father. The months since I left home have been agony. I wanted to tell him I was sorry. Now I'm too late, too late. Too late!"

Her voice trailed off in a flood of tears. Helen, the nurse, put her arm around the girl's trembling shoulders and sought to comfort her. "Hear, honey," she said softly, "is a note your father left on the bedside table. Maybe this will help."

Miriam seized the piece of yellow paper and read it eagerly.

"Thank God!" she gasped. "Thank God!"

Helen read the note the daughter held out to her. "My dearest Miriam, I forgive you. I pray you will also forgive me. I love you, too. Daddy."

"Forgiveness"—what a beautiful word! To be able to overlook faults and mistakes and to go on loving is a Christlike attribute essential to every Christian home.

Interestingly enough, the word *forgive* does not appear anywhere in Hosea's book. But who can deny that it is ever present in practically every chapter and every verse.

"Now you are mine!" "I will bind you to me forever." "I will betroth you to me in faithfulness and love." "I will wait for you" (Hosea 2:1, 19, 20; 3:3, TLB). Every word cries out "forgiveness." Every syllable declares, "I love you still! Come home! Stay with me!"

Forgiveness—tender, sincere, Christlike forgiveness—to cease being angry at some real or imagined act or word, to pardon the offender, to forgo any desire to punish husband, wife, son, daughter, brother, or sister—this is true forgiveness; this is the Jesus way.

"A more glorious victory cannot be gained over another man [or woman], than this, that when the injury began on [their] part, the kindness should begin on ours" a seventeenth-century archbishop of Canterbury once said.

Can you, do you, forgive?

Do You Have a Good Forgetter?

I have a book in my library entitled *How To Improve Your Memory.* A good book, it contains many helpful suggestions on an important subject. A good memory helps in every phase of life. But though I've never seen one on the subject, someone, somewhere, sometime, should write *How to Be a Good Forgetter.*

A photographic memory can be a tremendous asset. However, in a family questing for undimmed happiness, the blessing of forgetfulness is an absolute must.

Hosea was blessed with a good "forgetter." He had a lot that he needed to overlook if he was ever to bring Gomer back and put their home together. "She did a shameful thing" (Hosea 2:5, TLB). Here is the understatement of the Hosea-Gomer marital experience. Much of the first three chapters of Hosea's book is replete with her unsavory escapades. Gomer was selfish, sensual, and unfaithful. Hard, spiteful, seemingly impervious to appeals of love or reason, she cared nothing for the feelings of Hosea or their children. Even worse, she was probably involved in the fertility rites of Baal worship. It all added up to shattered love, heartbreak, tears, and desolation.

Yet Hosea was willing not only to forgive but to forget. "So I bought her [back]," he writes (Hosea 3:2). He was the husband who would forget the sleepless nights, the tortured thoughts, the stormy tantrums, the deceitful tongue, the base ingratitude, that created a wretched home for him and for the children in the family.

Love conquered all. Love forgave all. Love was willing to forget all.

The word *forget* appears only one time in the 14 chapters of Hosea's book. But it was a key to family reconciliation then, and it continues to play an important role in home happiness today. How much we need to forget any slights, any rebuffs, any unkind or hasty words, any mistakes—unintentional or otherwise. Love can still conquer. Still forgive. Still forget. And such forgetting will still help smooth the sometimes rocky road of matrimony. Try it if the occasion arises in *your* home. Be a Hosea!

Tiny carrot-topped Maria was right; it does take "a lot of loving" to be patient, forgiving, forgetting, and loyal in some families.

But a truly happy home is worth a Hosea-effort.

The Graying of Israel and Adventism

Advancing age doesn't always bring the golden years we read about. Listen to an Ann Landers correspondent who writes on the subject. "You know you are getting older when:

"Almost everything hurts. What doesn't hurt doesn't work any more.

"All the names in your little black book end in 'M.D.'

"Your knees buckle and your belt won't.

"You are 17 around the neck, 42 around the waist, and 126 around the golf course.

"You try to straighten the wrinkles in your socks and find you aren't wearing any.

"A little old gray-haired lady tries to help you across the street. She's your wife" (Ann Landers, Hendersonville, N.C., *Times-News*, Nov. 28, 1980).

Aging is a process of debilitation. Body functions deteriorate and mental performance may be less keen. For many, gray hair betrays the arrival of old age. Hosea uses graying of the hair to illustrate spiritual deterioration and apostasy among God's people. "Strangers have devoured his strength, and he knoweth it not: yea, gray hairs are here and there upon him, yet he knoweth not" (Hosea 7:9).

Israel was growing old and weak. Sin had sapped its

spiritual and national strength. "Their sins engulf them." "They commit falsehood." "The pride of Israel testifieth to his face." "They rebel against me." "Ephraim is a cake not turned." "Ephraim also is like a silly dove" (verses 2, NIV, 1, 10, 14, 8, 11).

Not a very pretty picture. A once strong and virile nation—now "graying"—its spiritual and political strength spent. Israel neared the end of its national existence.

What Caused the Gray Hairs?

Too close association with their pagan neighbors, socializing with those who knew not the Lord commenced the northern kingdom's downfall. "Ephraim, he hath mixed himself among the people" (verse 8). *The Living Bible* states, "My people mingle with the heathen, picking up their evil ways." "One of the chief reasons Israel apostatized was that they associated with the heathen and intermarried with them" *(The SDA Bible Commentary*, vol. 4, p. 907).

"It is God's purpose to manifest through His people the principles of His kingdom. That in life and character they may reveal these principles, He desires to separate them from the customs, habits, and practices of the world. He seeks to bring them near to Himself, that He may make known to them His will.

"This was His purpose in the deliverance of Israel from Egypt. . . . God desired to take His people apart from the world" *(Testimonies*, vol. 6, p. 9).

Mingling with the heathen and picking up their evil ways commenced the graying of Israel.

Loss of First Love

Israel lost its first love. "O Israel, how well I remember those first delightful days when I led you through the wilderness! How refreshing was your love! How satisfying, like the early figs of summer in their first season! But then you deserted me for Baal-peor, to give yourselves to other gods, and soon you were as foul as they" (Hosea 9:10, TLB).

Fraternizing with the world dulled Israel's perceptions of the omnipotence of Jehovah—His power and glory. Pleasures and pagan customs caused them to become confused in their obedience and worship of the living God.

Disregard for the Prophets

Israel turned its back upon God's word through His prophets and disregarded the admonitions and appeals of Moses, Elijah, Elisha, Amos, Isaiah, Micah, and His other inspired agents. "I appointed the prophets to guard my people," Hosea wrote, "but the people have blocked them at every turn and publicly declared their hatred, even in the Temple of the lord" (verse 8, TLB). "Hostility in the house of his God" awaited the prophets (NIV).

The prosperity of God's people depended upon their faithful adherence to the prophetic gift that He had placed among them. "Believe in the Lord your God, so shall ye be established; believe his prophets, so shall ye prosper" (2 Chron. 20:20).

Disregard for the gift accelerated the graying of Israel and her ultimate rejection as God's chosen people.

Israel Loses Its Vision of Mission

The Lord intended that His chosen evangelize their neighbors. He planned that Abraham and his descendants should take the knowledge of the true God to all parts of the known world. "In thee shall all families of the earth be blessed" (Gen. 12:3).

In Moses' day Israel was, by precept and example, to exalt His character (see Deut. 10:12). Through His chosen people God designed that His message of love and loyalty should reach out until all nations would learn of Him (see Deut. 12:20, first part; 28:8-10).

Only a holy people, reflecting God's holy law, could successfully win men and women to a holy God. By Hosea's day both Israel and Judah had grown so corrupt that they had forgotten the goal of world mission the Lord had placed before them.

Hosea rebukes Israel for its loss of vision, its deviation from God's goal as a missionary nation: "They are like a deceitful bow" (Hosea 7:16). "They are like a crooked bow that always misses targets" (TLB). Israel had missed the mark of its high calling. Instead of winning a pagan world to God, the pagans had led them to idolatry.

They Do Not Realize

Immersed in Baal orgies, Israel lived in a bizarre fantasy world. The frertility rites and sensuous religion of the people around them had corrupted their judgment and anesthetized their thinking. They viewed the God of Israel in the same way as their neighbors did Baal. Like their ancestors in Noah's day, they "knew not" the destruction awaiting them (Matt. 24:38, 39).

"He knoweth not" (Hosea 7:9). "They do not realize" (verse 2, NIV). The antediluvians and the Israel of Hosea's day shared the same delusion. As long as food and drink and pleasure were in abundance they felt

no pangs of conscience, no worrisome sense of inse-
curity. Everything was all right. God was pleased with
them. The graying of Israel proceeded apace without
their realizing what was happening—until it was too
late.

All this led Hosea to describe backsliding Israel as
"half-baked—scorched on one side and uncooked on
the other" (Hosea 7:8, Phillips). "This is a graphic
figure of spiritual inconsistency and inconstancy. The
Israelites were worshipers of the Lord by profession,
but engaged in the idolatries of the heathen" (The SDA
Bible Commentary, vol. 4, p. 907). Israel was nausating
to God—of no use to Him in its undone condition.

Thus was the graying of Israel becoming a sad
reality.

Paul would remind us, "Now all these things happened unto them for ensamples: and they are written
for our admonition, upon whom the ends of the world
are come" (1 Cor. 10:11).

For those, "upon whom the ends of the world are
come," inside the church as well as those with no
religious affiliations, Hosea's messages to Israel have
special significance. His warnings and appeals are for
us in our day.

The Graying of Adventism

Bear well in mind the contributing factors to the
graying of Israel: (1) too close association with the
world around it; (2) loss of its first love; (3) disregard
for the Spirit of Prophecy as manifested in its day; (4)
loss of vision of its God-given mission; (5) failure to
recognize its true condition before God. Do all or any
of these warning signals sound a message for Seventh-
day Adventists today?

Separation From the World

John's words to Christian believers of his day are as relevant to our own as they were to his: "Love not the world, neither the things that are in the world. If any man love the world, the love of the Father is not in him" (1 John 2:15).

The Lord's last-day messenger pens some thought-provoking words for us today: "The line of demarcation between worldlings and many professed Christians is almost indistinguishable. Many who once were earnest Adventists are conforming to the world—to its practices, its customs, its selfishness. Instead of leading the world to render obedience to God's law, the church is uniting more and more closely with the world in transgression. Daily the church is becoming converted to the world" *(Testimonies,* vol. 8, pp. 118, 119).

Ellen White wrote this many years ago. If she were here and witnessed some happenings in Seventh-day Adventist churches and institutions today, do you think she would write more favorably of our conduct?

Are Paul's words still as urgent as when he first wrote them to the Corinthian Christians: "Be ye not unequally yoked together with unbelievers: for what fellowship hath righteousness with unrighteousness? and what communion hath light with darkness? . . . Wherefore come out from among them, and be ye separate, saith the Lord, and touch not the unclean thing; and I will receive you" (2 Cor. 6:14-17).

Loss of First Love

Is the loss of our first love less prevalent among spiritual Israel today than it was in Hosea's day? Listen! "It is a solemn and terrible truth that many who have been zealous in proclaiming the third angel's message are now becoming listless and indifferent!" *(ibid.,* vol. 8, p. 118).

"The very first impulse of the renewed heart is to bring others also to the Saviour. Those who do not possess this desire give evidence that they have lost their first love; they should closely examine their own hearts in the light of God's word, and earnestly seek a fresh baptism of the Spirit of Christ" *(ibid.,* vol. 5, p. 386).

The True Witness writes, "Nevertheless I have somewhat against thee, because thou has left thy first love" (Rev. 2:4). Perhaps Christ's indictment of the church in Ephesus could as well apply to the church of Laodicea—the Seventh-day Adventist Church.

We dare not rest complacently upon our evangelistic laurels, as encouraging as they may be. We thank God for the thousand-a-day baptismal achievement. May God grant that this number may multiply many times before Jesus returns. And it will—when the latter rain falls upon God's converted people. But never forget, numbers are not the criteria by which God judges our success.

"If numbers were an evidence of success, Satan might claim the preeminence; for in this world his followers are largely in the majority. . . . It is the virtue, intelligence, and piety of the people composing our churches, not their numbers, that should be a source of joy and thankfulness" *(ibid.,* vol. 5, pp. 31, 32).

Does a diminishing zeal, a loss of first love reveal itself in our churches today? Is there a graying of Adventism?

Attitude Toward the Spirit of Prophecy

Satan has declared war on the remnant church (see Rev. 12:17) Why? The church not only keeps God's commandments that he hates, it also received the Spirit of Prophecy (Rev. 12:17; 19:10). The result of his antipathy toward the prophetic ministry? "There will be a hatred kindled against the testimonies which is satanic. The workings of Satan will be to unsettle the faith of the churches in them" *(Selected Messages,* book 1, p. 48).

Why is Satan so angry with the writings of God's messenger? "Satan cannot have so clear a track to bring in his deceptions and bind up souls in his delusions if the warnings and reproofs and counsels of the Spirit of God are heeded" *(ibid.).*

What is Satan doing? "Satan will work ingeniously, in different ways and through different agencies, to unsettle the confidence of God's remnant people in the true testimony" *(ibid.,* p. 48).

Efforts to weaken faith in the writings of Ellen White within the church today contribute to the graying of Adventism. Subtly and not so subtly Satan seeks to repeat what he did in Hosea's day. He is weakening confidence in God's gift of prophecy, encouraging closer ties with the world, a lowering of standards, a loss of first love—a drift toward apostasy. History is repeating itself.

These developments should awaken God's people. Read the next few words carefully: *"The very last deception of Satan* will be to make of none effect the testimony of the Spirit of God" *(Selected Messages,* book 1, p. 48; italics supplied).

Did you get that? *"The very last deception."* It suggests that what we are witnessing today may well be "the very last deception." We dare not delay our preparation for Jesus' soon return.

Are We Losing Our Vision of Mission?

How many members in your church are really on fire for the Lord? How many are zealously sharing their faith with others? Be honest now. Isn't only a small percentage of the membership doing most of the witnessing in your church? Are too many of us like "a crooked bow that always misses targets"? Are we losing our vision of mission? Why have we taken down the MV banners that used to read "The Advent Message to All the World in This Generation"?

"The true missionary spirit has deserted the churches that make so exalted a profession; their hearts are no longer aglow with love for souls and a desire to lead them into the fold of Christ" *(Testimonies,* vol. 4, p. 156).

We could go on. But should we? Shall we not rather go to our knees and rediscover the spirit of Jesus, the spirit of the pioneers, the spirit that will finish the work in our generation?

"Gray hairs are here and there upon him, *yet he knoweth it not"* (Hosea 7:9). How closely the words resemble God's last day message to Laodicea: "Because thou sayest, I am rich, and increased with goods, and have need of nothing; and *knowest not* that thou are wretched, and miserable, and poor, and blind, and naked" (Rev. 3:17).

"My brethren, you are disregarding the most sacred claims of God by your neglect to consecrate yourselves and your children to Him. Many of you are reposing in false security, absorbed in selfish interests, and attracted by earthly treasures. You fear no evil.

Danger seems a great way off. You will be deceived, deluded, to your eternal ruin unless you arouse and with penitence and deep humiliation return unto the Lord" *(ibid.,* vol. 5, p. 233).

Yet we are saying "All is well! We aren't so bad. In fact, we are doing quite well. Look at our statistics. Don't worry about us!" "I was shown that many are flattering themselves that they are good Christians, who have not a ray of light from Jesus" *(ibid.,* vol. 3, p. 253). Through it all—we *"know not."* We don't realize our true condition (Rev. 3:17).

"Never was there greater need of faithful warnings and reproofs . . . than at this very time" *(ibid.,* vol. 5, p. 676).

But the God of Israel still lives and will not leave us in our lukewarm, lost condition. Hope and help await the remnant people if we will but respond! "For there is hope of a tree, if it be cut down, that it will sprout again, and that the tender branch thereof will not cease" (Job 14:7). Just as the tree that is cut down "will sprout again," so there is glorious hope for the child of God who will respond to the tender appeals of a loving Saviour.

Hear these precious words—as much a part of the Laodicean message as the stinging rebukes for our lukewarmness: "Behold, I stand at the door, and knock: if any man hear my voice, and open the door, I will come in to him, and will sup with him, and he with me" (Rev. 3:20). While the message to Laodicea is a startling denunciation, it is also a message of assurance if we will respond to the Saviour's invitation.

"The counsel of the True Witness does not represent those who are lukewarm as in a hopeless case. There is yet a chance to remedy their state, and the

Laodicean message is full of encouragement" (E. G. White, in *Review and Herald,* Aug. 28, 1894).

What is that encouragement? "The backslidden church may yet buy the gold of faith and love, may yet have the white robe of the righteousness of Christ, that the shame of their nakedness need not appear. Purity of heart, purity of motive, may yet characterize those who are half-hearted and who are striving to serve God and Mammon. They may yet wash their robes of character and make them white in the blood of the Lamb" *(ibid.).*

Our case is not hopeless. The Laodician message contains a note of encouragement. There is still time. Modern day Mary Magdalenes, sinners like the thief on the cross—all of us still have opportunity. Jesus makes it possible.

"Blessed assurance, Jesus is mine!

O, what a foretaste of glory divine!

Heir of salvation, purchase of God,

Born of His Spirit, washed in His blood."

—Fanny J. Crosby, in *The SDA Hymnal,* No. 462.

By God's grace shall we not help turn the graying of Adventism into a power-filled greening of Adventism? By God's grace it can be done. By His Spirit it will be done. Ours is the "blessed" hope, not the "blasted" hope!

Prodigal, Come Home!

You have probably heard the story about Bill, who [was fed] up with the stodgy life at home.

"Dad," he said one day, "I'm tired of life around [here with my] sleepy parents. Give me my share of the estate now and let me go out and really live life."

Somewhat sadly Dad agreed to divide his wealth between [his sons. Bill] packed all his belongings and took [off for a distant land] and there wasted all his money [on wine and pros]titutes. Then his funds ran out, [leaving him]self stranded and penniless a long [way from home. In] desperation, he landed a job with [a farmer to f]eed his pigs. He was able to keep [body and soul to]gether by sharing the pigs' fare.

[Then Bill final]ly came to his senses. "Here I am dying [of hunger,]" he lamented to himself. "At home the hired [hands] eat better than I'm doing. I'm going home! I'll ta[ke] the rap and throw myself on Dad's mercy."

So Bill returned home. Ever since his son had left, his father had been anxiously watching the road leading up to the old home place. On that day Dad saw the familiar form come into view down by the lower 40. His heart skipped with expectation. In loving pity he ran and embraced his long-lost son and kissed him.

"Dad, I've been a rotter," Bill began.

"Quick!" the father cried to some of his servants.

"Bring the finest robe in the home and put it on him. And a jeweled ring for his finger. Be sure to bring some new shoes. Hurry out to the fattening pen and kill the best calf. We are going to celebrate. Bill was dead. Now he's alive again. He was lost and is found!"

"I will go home." "So he returned home." "He was dead; now he's alive."

Return! Return! Return!

Return—what a beautiful word. Under favorable circumstances, it calls forth all the tender emotions of home, mother, love. So it does when a sinner returns home—when a wanton wastrel becomes a child of God. When a prodigal wife returns to her husband. When a Laodicean church buys the gold of faith, puts on the white raiment of righteousness, and anoints its blind eyes with healing eyesalve.

Return—it is what Hosea appealed for his wife Gomer to do. It is what God urged wayward Israel to do. And it is what a Father of love still pleads with every erring child of Laodicea to do. "Return unto the Lord" (Hosea 6:1). This is what Hosea 6 and Revelation 3 are all about.

A Memorable Occasion

The 1973 Annual Council held in Takoma Park, Maryland, October 7-18, was an experience some of us will never forget. Dr. Herbert Douglass, at the time one of the *Review and Herald* editors, described it in the church paper as "different, exhilarating, and uncontrived."

"Simple words cannot convey adequately the mood and direction experienced by the 350 delegates at the 1973 Annual Council. But let it be said clearly, the issues raised, the concerns expressed, the urgencies shared, were not the usual agenda items to which church leaders have been accustomed during previous Annual Councils. In fact, these particular issues, concerns, and urgencies weren't even on the printed agenda—they moved in as men's hearts felt the leading of a greater Agenda Maker" (quoted in *Revival and Reformation,* p. 9).

Each morning, before the business sessions convened, prayer bands met in three General Conference office buildings. Others gathered in hotel and motel rooms and in private homes, praying for the spiritual welfare of individuals and for the church.

The one great burden of our hearts was "to make ready a people prepared for the Lord" (Luke 1:17). Longing to see Laodicea wake up, repent, and become zealous for the Christ of Revelation 3, we sought the Lord earnestly—that He would do something special for His leaders and members during the council. Weary of the "business as usual" approach to our yearly sessions, each one of us looked for something to happen that would kindle the fires of revival and reformation around the world.

During pre-council meetings church leaders meeting in administrative and department councils zeroed in on one theme—spiritual preparation for the final rapid movements that should bring "the blessed hope" of Titus 2:13 to early fruition.

At the close of this experience, the church leaders sent out an appeal to the worldwide church. It reflected the eager concern we all felt for revival and reformation within our ranks.

Hosea sums up the experience God longed for His wayward people to enter into: "Come, and let us return unto the Lord: for he hath torn, and he will heal us; he hath smitten, and he will bind us up" (Hosea 6:1). His heart yearned for Israel to forsake their sinful ways and return "home." The prophet's great desire was to see them return repentant, revived, and enjoying the rain of the Holy Spirit among them (see Hosea 6:2, 3).

It was also the burden of the leaders of God's church in October 1973. To return. To repent. To experience revival. To be prepared for the latter rain. God's call for revival and reformation during that Annual Council is as needful and as urgent as ever.

"We believe that the return of Jesus has been long delayed, that the reasons for the delay are not wrapped in mysteries, and that the primary consideration before the Seventh-day Adventist Church is to reorder its priorities individually and corporately so that our Lord's return may be hastened.

"We are not the first leaders in Adventist history to feel the urgency of preparing the church for the fullness of the 'latter rain' experience, the 'loud cry of the third angel's message,' and the triumphal return of the awaited Lord. Often God's special messenger to the remnant people made this appeal. Especially specific were her words written in 1892:

" 'The loud cry of the third angel has already begun in the revelation of the righteousness of Christ, the sin-pardoning Redeemer. This is the beginning of the light of the angel whose glory shall fill the whole earth' " (The SDA Bible Commentary, Ellen G. White Comments, vol. 7, p. 984). This statement is an inspired declaration that the fulfilling of Revelation 18:1-4, in which 'another angel' joins the three angels of Revelation 14:6-12 in lightening the whole earth with their glory, had begun. In the four years following the historic Minneapolis General Conference, the fresh, compelling emphasis on 'righteousness by faith' had aroused the Adventist Church in such a way that Ellen White could say that the 'loud cry' had begun!

"One question, therefore, has overshadowed all other subjects at this 1973 Annual Council: What has happened to the message and experience which by 1892 had brought the beginning of earth's final message of warning and appeal? . . .

"In attempting to find the specific present causes for failure and delay, the council has noted three main factors:

"1. Leaders and people have not fully accepted as a personal message, Christ's analysis and appeal to the Laodiceans (Rev. 3:14-22).

"2. Leaders and people are in some ways disobedient to divine directives, both in personal experience and in the conduct of the church's commission.

"3. Leaders and people have not yet finished the church's task" (*Autumn Council Actions*, 1973, pp. 3, 4).

Note carefully—church leaders were not laying responsibility for the Laodicean condition of the church upon the laity. We realized that we as leaders must share the accountability for the condition of the church. The appeal always includes the *leaders* as well as the *people*. We are all in this together.

Response to the Laodicean Message

"Becoming like Jesus in word and deed is the goal of the process called 'righteousness by faith': 'The righteousness of Christ is not a cloak to cover unconfessed and unforsaken sin; it is a principle of life that transforms the character and controls the conduct.

Holiness is wholeness for God; it is the entire surrender of heart and life to the indwelling of the principles of heaven' (*The Desire of Ages*, pp. 555, 556).

"As delegates to this Annual Council we believe that this is the heart of the church's need—understanding and experiencing all that is meant by the phrase, 'righteousness by faith.' Such righteousness is God's will lived out by continual faith in His power. God is waiting for a generation of Adventists who will demonstrate that His way of life can truly be lived on earth, that Jesus did not set an example beyond the reach of His followers, that his grace 'is able to keep you from falling and to present you without blemish' (Jude 24, RSV). . . .

"Every member . . . must recognize that he has a part in either hastening or delaying the coming of Christ. Says God's servant: 'When the character of Christ shall be perfectly reproduced in His people, then He will come to claim then as his own' (*Christ's Object Lessons*, p. 69)" (*Autumn Council Actions*, 1973, p. 5).

The report acknowledged that all is not well with us. It appealed for God's people to hear His voice of love, to return to Him, to repent of shortcomings, and to experience revival.

"As church leaders at this Annual Council we have faced honestly the fact that there are inconsistencies between the church's preaching and its practices, and that to allow these inconsistencies to continue will automatically delay the completion of the church's mission and the coming of Christ.

"God has in love sent to the Seventh-day Adventist Church inspired counsels that illuminate and apply the words of Scripture. These counsels cover about every conceivable facet of Christian experience and witness. As Seventh-day Adventists, we cannot plead ignorance of God's will concerning His expectations, either for the individual or for the church. If we ignore or reject God's counsels, this may well be defined as an act of insubordination, which will affect our relation to the coming of the Lord. In the words of God's servant: 'We may have to remain here in this world because of insubordination many more years, as did the children of Israel' *(Evangelism,* p. 696).

"At this Annual Council small study groups of church leaders have earnestly examined areas of possible failure to follow divine counsel. They have pointed up the need for greater care in Sabbath observance, in stewardship of God's gifts, in guarding the avenues of the soul, and in practicing the broad and specific principles of healthful living. On the latter question they have taken seriously the inspired statement: 'This is a work that will have to be done before His [God's] people can stand before Him a perfected people' *(Testimonies,* vol. 9, p. 154).

"These study groups also have pointed to evidences of sagging morality, including a more casual attitude toward divorce and remarriage. Concern has been expressed over the increasing tendency to imitate the world in dress and ornamentation.

"These study groups have examined the whole spectrum of Seventh-day Adventist institutional work and have pointed to evidences that some institutions in various respects are losing their distinctive character as instrumentalities for the furtherance of God's work on earth (see *Fundamentals of Christian Education,* p. 351).

"While earnest efforts have been made to reform, it

is recognized that as institutions grow larger, the difficulty of reforming is greater. . . .

"One of the greatest threats to our institutions of higher learning is seen in the counterfeit philosophies and theologies which may be unconsciously absorbed in worldly institutions by our future teachers and brought back as the 'wine' of Babylon to Adventist schools (see Rev. 14:8-10; 18:1-4). . . .

"As the Annual Council has reviewed these and other aspects of the lives of God's people and the institutions of the church, it has raised the question as to whether much of this represents insubordination to the authority and will of God so clearly expressed through His Word and the writings of the Spirit of Prophecy. Without attempting to pinpoint areas of insubordination, the Council pleads with God's people everywhere to respond to the appeal for revival and reformation—to make whatever changes may be necessary to enable the church to represent Christ adequately and fulfill its unique mission. . . .

" 'Had the purpose of God been carried out by His people in giving the world the message of mercy, Christ would ere this have come' *(Testimonies*, vol. 6, p. 450).

"God was willing to bring His work to a swift triumph following 1844, in 1888, and again in 1901 (among other times). Why then the delay? What can be done now?

"In response to this question, the delegates at this 1973 Annual Council extend the following appeal to all workers and members throughout the world. The appeal is threefold and yet it is one:

"1. Without further delay, open the heart's door fully to the waiting, pleading Saviour (Rev. 3:20). Admit

Jesus as the absolute Ruler of the life. Let Him enter the heart to transform it and to rule. Under the influence of the 'early rain,' live up to all the light you have. Put into practice all the counsel God has given you.

"2. Forsake the spirit of insubordination that too long has influenced individual and church decisions. This will prepare the way for the renewal of the 'latter rain' which has been delayed since the earlier years of our history, for God cannot send the Spirit in His fullness while people disregard the counsels He has graciously sent through that same Spirit, the Spirit of Prophecy.

"3. Make a new commitment to the church's task of reaching earth's billions with the three angels' messages. This commitment will call for personal dedication, for personal witnessing, for personal sacrifice. Moreover, it will call for deep intercession with God on the part of each member, a pleading with God for the 'latter rain' of the Holy Spirit's power for effectual, convincing, loving witness in deed and word.

God Has Great Things in Store

"We believe that all heaven is ready to do great exploits on behalf of the church that bears God's last call of mercy. We believe that God has wonderful surprises in store for every church member who commits himself completely to Heaven's plan for a perfected people—a people that will reflect the image of Jesus fully.

"That a genuine revival will come is clear from the following statement: 'Before the final visitation of God's judgments upon the earth, there will be, among the people of the Lord, such a revival of primitive godliness as has not been witnessed since apostolic times. The Spirit and power of God will be poured out upon His children' *(The Great Controversy*, p. 464). That Satan will endeavor to prevent this revival also is clear: 'The enemy of souls desires to hinder this work; and before the time for such a movement shall come, he will endeavor to prevent it, by introducing a counterfeit. In those churches which he can bring under his deceptive power he will make it appear that God's special blessing is poured out; there will be manifest what is thought to be great religious interest' *(ibid.)*. If the fast-spreading charismatic movement in the world today is the false revival forecast by God's Spirit, clearly the time must be near for God to pour out the latter rain upon His remnant people.

"Therefore, we appeal to our church members everywhere to join hands with the conference workers and church officers in a great revival and reformation that will enable God to reveal His power and glory to a needy, desperate world. With all the solemnity that we can command, we appeal to every member to study God's Word earnestly, to seek first the kingdom of God and His righteousness, and to pray for the outpouring of the Holy Spirit for a finished task (see *Testimonies to Ministers*, pp. 506-512).

"Time is short. 'Therefore be ye also ready: for in such an hour as ye think not the Son of man cometh' (Matt. 24:44; see also *Testimonies*, vol. 6, p. 406; *Selected Messages*, book 1, p. 67)" *(Autumn Council Actions*, 1973, pp. 5-8).

As Hosea appealed to Israel 800 years before Christ, so the Holy Spirit pleads with His people today. He implores us to repent, to return to Him, to experience true revival and reformation, in preparation for the outpouring of the Holy Spirit in Pentecostal power. This is what Hosea's book is all about. It is as urgently applicable as it was in his day. The possible return of Jesus in our day makes it so. "Come, let us return to the Lord; it is he who has torn us—he will heal us. He has wounded—he will bind us up" (Hosea 6:1, TLB).

Shall we not say with the prodigal "I will go home!"

> "I've wandered far away from God,
> Now I'm coming home;
> The paths of sin too long I've trod;
> Lord, I'm coming home. . . .
> Open wide thine arms of love;
> Lord, I'm coming home."

> —William J. Kirkpatrick,
> in *The SDA Hymnal*, No. 296.

Needed: Strong Last-Day Leaders!

"How do you like civilian life?" someone asked a newly retired naval officer.

"It's terrible," the old vet replied sourly. "All these people running around, and nobody in charge!"

God's last-day army needs "somebody in charge." It was for this reason He early organized His people by thousands, hundreds, fifties, and tens (Ex. 18:25). Moses then selected men from all Israel to serve "as leaders" over these units (verse 25, TEV).

In the beginning Israel's leaders were "able men, such as fear God, men of truth, hating coveteousness" (Ex. 18:21). As time passed, the influence of pagan neighbors corrupted them. They turned their backs upon God, slipping into the fertility religions of the tribes about them. By Hosea's day He denounced both people and leaders. "They have set up kings, but not by me: they have made princes, and I knew it not" (Hosea 8:4). "Without my consent; . . . without my approval" (NIV).

"During the 250 years that the northern kingdom lasted, the throne was occupied by six or more wretched dynasties, and by 19 unhappy monarchs, all of whom were apostate from God and tyrants over the people. None of the kings of the 10 tribes did Jehovah recognize as His viceregent" (*The Pulpit Commentary,* vol. 30, p. 251).

False Religion

Apostate leaders drew the people into idolatry. "Of their silver and their gold have they made them idols. . . . Thy calf . . . hath cast thee off. . . . The workman made it; therefore it is not God" (Hosea 8:4-6).

Jeroboam set up images in Bethel and in Dan. The northern kingdom instructed its people to worship the golden bulls within their own borders rather than go to the Temple in Jerusalem. The golden bulls would represent Jehovah to them. Also Israel installed a priesthood other than the designated Levites and created a whole new system of worship. The products of men's hands became the objects of worship. Images replaced the living God. The idols in Bethel and Dan became the centers of the new system. Gross apostasy swept through the northern kingdom. Hosea devoted much of his ministry to relaying God's displeasure and indictment of Israel because of its idol worship. Both Hosea and Amos inveighed strongly against the mixing of pagan and true religion and declared it spiritual adultery.

Pagan Allies

Evil leaders led the nation further toward the brink of disaster. They turned to their pagan neighbors for help instead of appealing to Jehovah. "Ephraim hath hired lovers" (Hosea 8:9). "They call to Egypt, they go to Assyria" (Hosea 7:11). Expediency and compromise became the policy of declining Israel. More and more its deluded leaders depended upon pagan gods and allies.

False Altars

God also had a controversy with Israel over false

LCH-5

altars. "Ephraim hath made many altars, . . . altars shall be unto him to sin" (Hosea 8:11). A paraphrase renders the passage as "Ephraim has built many altars, but they are not to worship me! They are altars of sin" (TLB). "Her people love the ritual of their sacrifice, but to me it is meaningless" (verse 13, TLB).

Altars in ancient Israel were intended to be part of the worship of the living God. Built to deal with sin, they instead became places where the people indulged in the sensual celebrations of pagan fertility rites. Structures intended to cleanse from sin became centers for sin itself.

Israel did not turn from religion. People had more zeal for it than before. But it was a corrupt worship. It all was nauseating to the God of heaven.

Israel continued to erect altars "on every high hill and any other place that pleased them. This multiplication of altars had the appearance of religion, but only the appearance" *(The Pulpit Commentary,* vol. 30, p. 249). The people of Israel were guilty of forgetting their Creator (see Hosea 8:14).

False Security

As both the northern kingdom and Judah departed from God they sought to build up their own defenses to provide security against potential attackers. "For Israel hath forgotten his Maker, and buildeth temples; and Judah hath multiplied fenced cities" (verse 14).

Israel's false leaders lured the nation into a sense of false security. Perhaps they sought to convince the people that they could depend upon the efforts of their hands to save them from the enemy. God spared no effort to convince them they were following a dangerous illusion. "I will send a fire upon his cities, and it shall devour the palaces thereof" (verse 14).

Commenting on this verse, James Montgomery Boice says: "The word translated 'palaces' is 'spacious' or 'bigness . . . ' The central idea of 'bigness.' What God is talking about in these phrases is the passion of the nation at that time to build big things. Having forsaken God, who alone is big enough for her need, Israel tried to compensate by the construction of big things without Him" *(The Minor Prophets,* pp. 58, 59).

It is easy to become obsessed with bigness. We should never fear big things or great accomplishments. Our God is limitless in His ability to provide for His people. Smallness is no assurance of piety. On the other hand, we need to beware of any parallel assumption that just because a building, a project, a statistic, or a plan is big in its scope, it must follow that it is heaven-blessed.

Leaders in Israel had "forgotten the law" (Hosea 4:6). They had rejected God's knowledge (Hosea 4:6; 5:4). Truth had been corrupted and abandoned (Hosea 4:1). Removing the landmarks (Hosea 5:10, NKJV), they worshiped idols and were "stubborn" (Hosea 4:16, NKJV). Israel failed—miserably failed—in their God-given task of representing God to the nations around them.

Why? Largely because Israel's leaders were not fully consecrated to the living God and to the principles for which He stood. They "set up kings, but not by me" (Hosea 8:4). What a sad lament on a people that God had destined to be "the head" and not the tail (see Deut. 28:44).

Strong Seventh-day Adventist Leaders Needed Today!

From Israel's experience, God would have His people today learn valuable lessons. The success of any organization is, under God, dependent upon its leadership. We need now, more than ever, strong leaders, committed to Christ, the message, and the goals of His last-day church. Men and women—leaders—are more important than policies and budgets.

On every level of church leadership we must have Adventism's finest, most committed, most capable. The local churches, the conferences, the departments, the institutions all the way through to the General Conference, deserve loyal, efficient, incorruptible men and women. No less will suffice for God's last-day movement. Our leaders must have an "understanding of the times, to know what Israel ought to do" (1 Chron. 12:32).

We need leaders who not only "know" but who are also able to "do" what needs to be done. They must be well trained and well qualified wherever they serve. Academically and practically, they must have the qualifications needed for whatever post God places them in—but the Seventh-day Adventist Church is no cold, calculating business corporation, nor should it be operated as such. We need carefully considered, viable policies, safe and sound business procedures administered by efficient men and women—of course! Such indispensables are presuppositions for denominational achievement—but—impeccable academic training is not enough. Congenial, personal relationships by themselves will not suffice. Nor will sound judgment and productive skills. The church needs more than reliable financial acumen or keen, knowl egeable managerial ability. Each of these enviable assets is laudable, desirable, and maybe absolutely essential. But these *alone* will never make a successful Seventh-day Adventist leader today. These are priceless, but if the qualifications end there, something is missing.

We hear much about IQ—the intelligent quotient. In the selection of leaders in God's work, IQ is important, but the SQ is even more so. The spiritual quotient is absolutely indispensable in the selection of Seventh-day Adventist leaders. If God's church is to measure up to His standard of achievement, the spiritual quotient must be the major factor.

Before proceeding further, we should be clear on one point. When God speaks of leaders and workers, He includes both men and women. He has a ministry for every member (see Mark 13:34). "The Lord has a work for women as well as men to do" *(Testimonies,* vol. 6, p. 117). Both the Old and New Testaments have many references to women involved in prophetic, liturgical, and social ministries. But as we advance in this area, we must make sure that we base all our decisions on the Bible and the counsel of Ellen White and not just follow the example of other denominations.

Twentieth-Century Gods

The world has many false gods. Wealth, knowledge, pleasure, friends—the list is almost endless. Too many people in our day replace the God of heaven by things in this life. Materialism—the amassing of wealth, the enjoyment of that which it can buy— becomes the God of many. The philosophy that places man and the works of his hand above the Creator—

humanism—is a well-known god in our day. The rejection or exclusion of religious consideration, the acceptance of only that which pertains to earthly values—secularism—becomes the god of more millions. It results in humanity's feeling no need of the true God.

God says to present-day spiritual Israel what He told His people in Hosea's day: "They were counted as a strange thing" (Hosea 8:12). "The Lord accepteth them not; now will he remember their iniquity, and visit their sins" (verse 13). "They have sown the wind, and they shall reap the whirlwind" (verse 7).

Modern people need some modern Hoseas—leaders—to warn and save them from modern gods as much as ancient Israel did. Today's Adventist church leaders must be prepared to meet this challenge.

Twentieth-Century Allies

It is not easy for Adventist leaders in the local churches, the conferences, the institutions, or in the General Conference to hold the line against the world and its allurements or to hold up the standards that make us a different people. Yet the apostle Peter reminds us, "Ye are a chosen generation, a royal priesthood, an holy nation, a peculiar people; that ye should shew forth the praises of him who hath called you out of darkness into his marvellous light" (1 Peter 2:9).

Expediency easily becomes the policy in our day. It follows a course of action that offers temporary advantage without regard for principle. A path of least resistance, it leads to compromise. On occasion it slips into modern administration even in our own church committees and boards.

It's so easy to yield just a little, to
adjustment (we must not call it "c(
is a bad word). We "deemphasize'
promise" when we opt for an expedient wa᷉y ᷉
can live with this," we tell ourselves with relief; "wᴇ
can 'go along' with this solution."

It is not only in our medical or education programs,
by any means, that we sometimes resort to expediency. Preachers can be guilty, too! It is much easier to
speak on peace, love, and charity than it is to call sin
by its right name. We think we are keeping peace and
harmony during a board or committee meeting by
"sitting on our hands" instead of standing on our feet
to be counted.

God challenges today's Adventist leaders, as he did
those in Hosea's day, to remain true to the principles
that set us apart as a peculiar people.

Expediency is an appealing crutch. It not only
persuades us to accept easier answers inside the
church, but on occasion it may also lure us to make
inappropriate allies outside. Today our leaders are
under some subtle pressure from ecumenical and
evangelical sources to reconcile our differences. "Why
do you have to be so different? Why can't you tone
down some of your peculiar doctrinal positions? We
could live with you in Christian fellowship and cooperate with you if you would do this!"

Adventist leaders must have the courage to with-
stand the blandishments of Babylon today as our
pioneers did a century ago. The bewitching siren call
of total Christian unity is attractive and a real danger
to God's people today. Our Assyrias, our Egypts,
sometimes take the form of worldly approbation or of
ecumenism, a quest for the approval of other

churches and their leaders. If we give a little here and there, we may find allies that prove our undoing just as Israel discovered in Hosea's day.

We must relate in a winning way to the world and to other Christians but never forsake the unique mission entrusted to us as God's last-day people. We have a message to preach, a task to perform—something we must never lose sight of. No allies of convenience must cause us to deviate from our divinely appointed assignments.

Spurious Altars Today

Corrupt altars in Hosea's day were a symbol of an insidious, encrouching formalism. The religion of the northern kingdom laid great emphasis upon rites and ceremonies. It substituted ritual for godly living and wholehearted commitment to Jehovah. God warns His remnant church against such modern altars—such dry formalism.

"Personal religion among us as a people is at a low ebb. There is much form, much machinery, much tongue religion; but something deeper and more solid must be brought into our religious experience" *(Testimonies,* vol. 5, p. 743).

Formalism "is of the head, and deals with externals. It stops with the theory of religion. It goes no deeper than the form and the pretense. Hence it is like salt without savor. It is a joyless, loveless religion, for it does not bring peace, assurance, and victory. . . . It is one of those subtle, all-pervading evils which the Redeemer came to uproot and eliminate from the human heart" (A. G. Daniells, *Christ Our Righteousness,* pp. 75, 76).

"The same danger still exists. Many take it for

granted that they are Christians, simply because they subscribe to certain theological tenets. But they have not brought the truth into practical life. They have not believed and loved it, therefore they have not received the power and grace that come through sanctification of the truth. Men may profess faith in the truth; but if it does not make them sincere, kind, patient, forbearing, heavenly-minded, it is a curse to its possessors, and through their influence it is a curse to the world" (*The Desire of Ages*, pp. 309, 310).

God calls upon His people today to replace mere perfunctory adherence to formal piety with a deep heartfelt experience whose wellspring is a warm abiding love for Christ and all that He stands for. God's leaders today are to lend their example and efforts to assure that God's remnant does not itself rear spurious altars of formalism.

False Security

False gods, false allies, false altars, must provide no false security for modern Seventh-day Adventists. An easy life, freedom from God-given standards, or freedom from sacrifice and service have never characterized God's planning for His people. Freedom from the claims of a love-inspired obedience to God's holy law never has been, or ever will be, a part of true Seventh-day Adventist theology.

We must maintain the doctrinal integrity of the church. Forces, both overt and subtle, will seek to undermine the pillars of our faith. "For I know this, that after my departing shall grievous wolves enter in among you, not sparing the flock" (Acts 20:29). "Satan himself is transformed into an angel of light. Therefore it is no great thing if his ministers also be transformed as the ministers of righteousness" (2 Cor. 11:14, 15).

"Satan and his angels are making every effort to obtain control of minds, that men may be swayed by falsehood and pleasing fables" (*Selected Messages*, book 1, p. 194).

"This reformation would consist of giving up the doctrines which stand as the pillars of our faith, and engaging in a process of reorganization. Were this reformation to take place, what would result? The principles of truth that God in His wisdom has given to the remnant church, would be discarded. Our religion would be changed. The fundamental principles that have sustained the work for the last 50 years would be accounted as error" (*ibid.*, p. 204).

To face the difficult days ahead for God's church will require leaders with two essential qualities—great *wisdom* to know *what* to do and *courage* to *do* it. During this crucible of testing "many a star that we have admired for its brilliancy will then go out in darkness" (*Testimonies*, vol. 5, p. 81).

Every officer in this church is important—from those who lead the local churches right up through the General Conference. We should determine to have every office filled with born-again leaders who believe and preach the full message that has made us a people—the three angels' messages, the sanctuary, sanctification as well as justification, the validity of the law of God, the gift of prophecy in the remnant church manifest in the ministry of Ellen White, the imminent return of Christ—the whole gamut. *This is Adventism.*

"Men of stamina are wanted, men who will not wait to have their way smoothed and every obstacle removed, men who will inspire with fresh zeal the flagging efforts of dispirited workers, men whose hearts are warm with Christian love and whose hands are strong to do their Master's work" *(The Ministry of Healing,* p. 497).

"The greatest want of the world is the want of men—men who will not be bought or sold, men who in their inmost souls are true and honest, men who do not fear to call sin by its right name, men whose conscience is as true to duty as the needle to the pole, men who will stand for the right though the heavens fall" *(Education,* p. 57).

God, give us such leaders for our day!

Beware, Lest Thou Forget

On November 7, 1985, Elder David Baasch was acting chairman of the Thursday morning General Conference Committee. During his devotional study Baasch posed a thought-provoking question. He was commenting on an article in a secular magazine that dealt with the rise of several pagan religions between 700 and 500 B.C. A span that includes Hosea's prophetic career in Israel.

"During this period," Elder Baasch said, "Buddhism, Confucianism, Shintoism, and some other Oriental religions came into being. Through the centuries many millions of people have espoused these faiths. These bulwarks of paganism today comprise the majority of the great groups of unreached peoples that the church is seeking to reach during Harvest 90."

Then comes the question worth pondering: "One might question, If Israel had been true to her charge to be the light of the world and faithfully taken the message of Jehovah, the living God, to this area of the world—would there be great masses of pagan peoples in these areas today?

"As Israel had the answer to the heart-longings of people in their time, so God's church today has the answer for the needs of modern man. May God help us to give a spiritual message that will elevate minds to the exalted and satisfying themes of reconciliation and eternal life."

Worth thinking about, isn't it?

Three central thoughts rivet our attention: (1) the danger of forgetting the way Jehovah has led His people, (2) the sad reminder of what might have been in the history of Israel if they had been faithful to God, and (3) His challenge for a wholehearted commitment to Him.

Gilgal—Place of Dishonor

"All their wickedness is in Gilgal; for there I hated them: for the wickedness of their doings . . ." (Hosea 9:15).

Gilgal was a place of rebellion: Here Israel rebelled against God as their sovereign king (1 Sam. 11:14, 15). God was to be Israel's ruler. The people, in their sin, demanded a human leader so they could be like the nations about them. Through the prophet Samuel God warned the people of their mistaken demands and the burden that they would stagger under if they insisted on having a king (1 Sam. 8:5-21). Still they persisted, and He yielded to their demands; but they paid a high price for their rebellion.

Gilgal was a place of presumption: Here King Saul officiated at the altar where only God's priests were to preside. Israel was going into battle with the Philistines. Samuel did not arrive in time to seek God's blessing and presence, so Saul proceeded to offer the sacrifice. By his act he forfeited the privilege of founding a dynasty (1 Sam. 13:13, 14).

Gilgal was a place of disobedience: God instructed Saul that in his war with the Amalakites he was to "utterly destroy all that they have, and spare them not; but slay both man and woman, infant and suckling, ox and sheep, camel and ass" (1 Sam. 15:3). The king did not follow the Lord's command; he spared King Agag and certain animals.

Gilgal was a place of rejection: "The Spirit of the Lord departed from Saul, and an evil spirit from the Lord troubled him" (1 Sam. 16:14). It was a sad day when his rebellion, his presumption, and his disobedience led to the Lord's rejecting and withdrawing His Spirit from Saul.

Finally, *Gilgal was a place of the hated idol worship:* It became a center where the kings of the northern kingdom after Jeroboam came to worship in a mixture of pagan and true religon (Hosea 4:15; 9:15; 12:11; Amos 4:4; 5:5).

What Might Have Been

Gilgal might have been a place of honor for God's chosen people. The site had been the scene of God's power for His love and care for Israel. God performed a miracle for His people at Jordan. He halted the waters of the turbulent river so people "passed over on dry land" (Joshua 3:17). To commemorate the event, God instructed that they should erect an altar with stones from the riverbed (Joshua 4:3). "And the people came up out of Jordan . . . , and encamped in Gilgal. . . . And those twelve stones, which they took out of Jordan, did Joshua pitch in Gilgal" (verses 19, 20). Gilgal might have been a perpetual reminder of God's wonder-working power.

Gilgal was a symbol of God's deliverance. "Israel served Eglon the king of Moab eighteen years" (Judges 3:14). When the people cried to the Lord for deliverance, "the Lord raised them up a deliverer, Ehud, the son of Gera" (verse 15). It was at Gilgal that Ehud killed

Eglon as he sat alone in his palace parlor (see verses 20-23).

Gilgal was the location of one of the schools of the prophets. Here young men were able "to gain an education that would lead them to magnify the law and make it honorable. . . . Especially did . . . [Elijah] instruct them concerning their high privilege of loyally maintaining their allegiance to the God of heaven. He also impressed upon their minds the importance of letting simplicity mark every feature of their education" *(Prophets and Kings,* pp. 224, 225). The place might have developed into a strong religious education center but for the apostasy of Israel.

Gilgal's history could be summed up in four melancholy words: "It might have been." Inspired history expands the lament: "All their wickedness in Gilgal: for there I hated them: for the wickedness of their doings I will drive them out of mine house, I will love them no more" (Hosea 9:15).

God's people today dare not lightly pass over Israel's sad experiences at Gilgal. Perhaps we have had our own Gilgal. Perhaps Heaven laments the sad shortcomings of the church at the 1888 General Conference session in Minneapolis.

A. G. Daniells, former president of the General Conference, later wrote about the session: "The message of Righteousness by Faith came clear and fully into the open. . . . It was made the one great subject of study in the devotional part of the Conference. . . . How sad, how deeply regrettable, it is that this message of righteousness in Christ should, at the time of its coming, have met with opposition on the part of earnest, well-meaning men in the cause of God! The message has never been received, nor proclaimed, nor given free course as it should have been in order to convey to the church the measureless blessings that were wrapped within it" *(Christ Our Righteousness,* pp. 41-47).

Ellen White observed, "Had the purpose of God been carried out by His people in giving to the world the message of mercy, Christ would, ere this, have come to the earth, and the saints would have received their welcome into the city of God" *(Testimonies,* vol. 6, p. 450).

What "might have been" in our own church history is worth our prayerful consideration a century later.

Through Hosea God reflects upon Israel's history. It contained both joy and victory, disaster and defeat. Through it all He had led and supported His people. "O, Israel, how well I remember those first delightful days when I led you through the wilderness! How refreshing was your love! . . . But then you deserted me for Baal-peor, to give yourself to other gods, and soon you were as foul as they" (Hosea 9:10, TLB).

In their long journey from Egyptian bondage God guided His chosen people over miles of miracles. They had experienced the deliverance from the plagues of Egypt (Ex. 7-12) and the supernatural rolling back of the Red Sea (Ex. 14:21). God provided manna—food— and water in the desert (Ex. 16:14, 31; 15:25). The Lord manifested His presence to Israel, in a cloud by day and a pillar of fire by night (Ex. 13:21). Israel heard the voice of God at Sinai (Ex. 19, 20). Every day, week in and week out, evidences of God's love and blessing surrounded them.

Now they stood on the borders of Canaan, an unseen, untried way ahead. This new generation of Israelites were about to inherit a land "flowing with milk and honey." It was a sharp contrast to the privations of the past.

To help them face the unknown, to fortify them against the temptations of the future, God had a message for them: "Beware lest thou forget the Lord!" To strengthen them for whatever the future held as they stood on the borders of the Promised Land, God reminded them of His past blessings and leadership.

Unfortunately, Israel did not remember long. In his day Hosea declared, "Israel hath forgotten his Maker" (Hosea 8:14). The northern kingdom had turned to other gods. Again in the opening verses of Hosea 9 God reflects upon Israel's history.

For Us Today

God's message for His people standing on the borders of the eternal promised land today is "Beware lest thou forget the Lord!" The Lord's last-day messenger echoes Moses' words in modern speech: "We have nothing to fear for the future, except as we shall forget the way the Lord has led us, and His teaching in our past history" (*Life Sketches*, p. 196).

Miracles of God's leadership filled the early years of Adventism. The leading of the Holy Spirit appears in days of study and nights of prayer, in organization—departmental and geographic—in locating sites for key institutions in America, Australia, and other lands.

In the early 1940s I was a young pastor of the Takoma Park church. In those days it had the reputation as the General Conference church since many of the world church leaders worshiped there. In my congregation were such denominational stalwarts as Elders W. A. Spicer, W. W. Prescott, I. H. Evans, F. C. Gilbert, C. S. Longacre, H. H. Votaw, Carlyle B. Haynes, and others. It stirred and warmed my heart as they recounted the miracles and blessings of those early days.

As Seventh-day Adventists we indeed "have nothing to fear for the future, except as we shall forget the way the Lord has led us, and His teaching in our past history."

This was the message Hosea endeavored to impress upon Israel in his day (Hosea 9:10). Unfortunately, his efforts were largely in vain, "for Israel hath forgotten his Maker" (Hosea 8:14). Where ancient Israel failed, God's spiritual Israel in our day must not. "His teaching in our past history" must ever be fresh in our minds.

Challenge to Wholehearted Commitment

Israel was not wholly on God's side. "Their heart is divided" (Hosea 10:2). While they paid lip service to Jehovah, they also worshiped other gods. "They feared the Lord, and served their own gods, after the manner of the nations whom they carried away from thence" (2 Kings 17:33).

Jehovah God does not accept divided hearts— conflicting loyalties. In Hosea's day and in ours He asks wholehearted devotion. "Ye shall seek me, and find me, when ye shall search for me with all your heart" (Jer. 29:13).

"The whole heart must be yielded to God, or the change can never be wrought in us by which we are to be restored to His likeness. By nature we are alienated from God. The Holy Spirit describes our condition in such words as these: 'Dead in trespasses and sins'; 'the whole head is sick, and the whole heart faint'; 'no soundness in it.' We are held fast in the snare of Satan;

'taken captive by him at his will' (Eph. 2:1; Isa. 1:5, 6; 2 Tim. 2:26). God desires to heal us, to set us free. But since this requires an entire transformation, a renewing of our whole nature, we must yield ourselves wholly to Him" (*Steps to Christ*, p. 43).

The Saviour makes it clear we cannot be loyal to God and to a sinful world at the same time. "No man can serve two masters: for either he will hate the one, and love the other; or else he will hold to the one, and despise the other. Ye cannot serve God and mammon" (Matt. 6:24).

God's appeal to His church today is the same as in Hosea's and Jesus' day—wholehearted, undivided consecration to Him and to the finishing of His work.

The Gospel of Hosea

Hosea pauses in a Samaritan slave market, surveying the scene. His beloved Gomer is about to be sold into slavery. Tears well in his eyes.

The bidding is brisk.

"Ten shekels!" a voice cries.

"Make it 11," another bawls.

The prophet stands speechless for a moment. Should he love her or loathe her? It all seemed so easy from a distance. But now he is face-to-face with his moment of truth.

"Make it 12!" a coarse voice croaks.

"Thirteen!" "Fourteen!" others bid.

Hosea struggles to rouse himself from his stunned stupor.

"Fifteen shekels!" "Fifteen and a half!"

It will soon be too late!

He pushes forward toward the auction platform. "Make way! Make way!" he bellows as he shoulders his way through the bidders. Waving his arms frantically, he cries, "Add a homer and half of barley to that 15 shekels!"

Heads turn. Who is this who bids so wrecklessly? Startled voices whisper, "It's Hosea!" "It's her husband!"

Gomer too hears the familiar voice.

She looks up, her eyes meeting his. Shame overwhelms her. Her gaze drops. Why has he come? To mock her? To scorn her? Perhaps even to kill her?

The bidding ceases. Once again Gomer belongs to Hosea. At first by marriage, now by redemption. He has bought her back.

Five words tell the gospel story of Hosea as he stood that day by the Samaritan slave platform. "So I bought her [back]" (Hosea 3:2).

Usually we think of Isaiah as the gospel prophet, since his book contains prophecies of the coming Messiah. Isaiah 53 particularly contains a most impassioned description of God's love and sacrifice. But Hosea, likewise, could be called a "gospel prophet." His marital experience and his inspired pen both describe the good news of God's love and redemption. Gomer falls into sin and degradation. Hosea loves and forgives her. Buying her back from the slavery of sin, he nurtures her to faith and obedience. He writes of a deliverance from sin that will be forever. The whole blessed good news flows freely from his pen. Better still, it is lived out in his life and his relationship with Gomer.

Gomer's sin was of the darkest hue. The prophet describes her as one who has "done shamefully," who has "played the harlot" (Hosea 2:5). "An adulteress" (Hosea 3:1), a "wife of whoredoms" (Hosea 1:2), she looked "to other gods" and loved "flagons of wine" (Hosea 3:1). She went after other lovers (Hosea 2:5).

In her sinful condition Gomer desperately needed help. Not only did she experience shame, abandonment, and slavery; she faced eternal death, "the wages of sin" (Rom. 6:23). She urgently required the gospel.

Laodicean Stupor

God's last-day messenger sees His remnant church

in need of the gospel to arouse her from Laodicean stupor. "It is a sad picture—the feeble piety, the want of consecration and devotion to God. There has been a separation of the soul from God" (Ellen G. White, in *Review and Herald Extra*, Dec. 23, 1890).

"The church has turned back from following Christ her Leader and is steadily retreating toward Egypt. Yet few are alarmed or astonished at their want of spiritual power" *(Testimonies*, vol. 5, p. 217).

Gomer had to have the gospel. Ancient Israel needed it. The world lacks the gospel. We, as spiritual Israel today, require it. The book of Hosea reveals this precious good news most beautifully.

The gospel declares that lost sinners pursuing sin may become redeemed saints running away from sin. "The Son of Man is come to seek and to save that which is lost" (Luke 19:10). Thank God, there is no sin—however despicable—from which the gospel of the Lord Jesus Christ cannot save a penitent transgressor.

Help and Hope for All

Sin is the ugly monster from which all must be saved. The Bible describes it in many ways. It is breaking God's commandments (1 John 3:4), contempt for others (Prov. 14:21), foolish thinking (Prov. 24:9), vain talk (Prov. 10:19), unbelief (Rom. 14:23). Sin is "all unrighteousness" (1 John 5:17).

Thank God for the promise: "Thou shalt call his name Jesus: for he shall save his people from their sins" (Matt. 1:21). Notice well that Jesus *can* and *must* save us *from* our sins—not *in* them. Any alleged gospel that does not deliver the sinner from the *power* of sin, as well as from its *guilt*, is not the good news God has for sinners.

The gospel of love *de*nounces sin, *pro*nounces doom, and *an*nounces redeeming love for all who will accept God's provision. Benjamin Franklin once said, "Sin is not hurtful because it is forbidden, but it is forbidden because it is hurtful." The gospel takes care of it all.

Gomer sinned against Hosea. She did not deserve love and compassion, but instead punishment. Yet patient, tenderhearted Hosea loved her and longed to save her from herself. "I will allure her" he declared (Hosea 2:14). "I will do everything within my power to win her back."

"I will have mercy upon her," Hosea said (verse 23). Mercy is an act of divine favor. Gomer needed mercy. Every sinner requires it. Hosea, as a type or symbol of God, was ready to extend mercy to his wayward wife. The prophet's book is, as one writer says, "one long impassioned monologue, broken by sobs." Hosea was prepared to go to any lengths to save her.

God has a plan to win back His erring children. Called the plan of redemption, it was born in the heart of God long before Gomer's day. The gospel is "the hidden wisdom, which God ordained before the world unto our glory" (1 Cor. 2:7). Jesus is "the Lamb slain from the foundation of the world" (Rev. 13:8). Hosea reveals through both precept and example God's desire to save Gomer and Israel.

Love Is the Catalyst

Love inspired God's plan to save us. Hosea's love shines through in all of his relationships with Gomer. He appeals to his children to beg their mother to give up her life of sin, to come back home to her lawful husband and to her family. "Plead with your mother, plead," he entreats (Hosea 2:2). Hosea is faithful to Gomer in spite of her abandonment of him. The word of the Lord ever rebuked him when he wavers. He was told to show his love to his wife again. The charge obsessed him (Hosea 3:1).

After all appeals fail, see Hosea's constant affection when he discovers Gomer slouched in a Samaritan slave market. There she stands, haggard, bereft— about to be sold into slavery. The face that once glowed in radiant loveliness is gray and wrinkled. Once well-coiffed hair is streaked with gray and falls in stringy wisps over tear-stained cheeks. Eyes that once danced with vibrant life, appeal for sympathy. Hosea's love is tested to its utmost. What shall he do with this hapless outcast? Is she to be pitied or blamed? His heart goes out to her in compassion. The prophet still loves her, still wants her home where she belongs. Instantly he decides that he will buy her back, whatever the price. He will take her home again.

God sent the prophet on his mission of love to reveal His limitless affection for Israel. Through his experience you and I catch a faint glimmer of that love as it reaches out for the lost. As He dispatched Hosea on his redemptive mission to reclaim Gomer and to arouse Israel, so He sends His Holy Spirit to transform careless Laodicean hearts today. He still loves. He still cares. He still saves.

Try, if you are able, to picture the poignant scene as Jesus leaves the courts of God to become a babe in a human womb. Imagine the parting scene as the Son of God bids farewell to His Father and to the angel host. They know well what lies ahead on our sinful planet for their beloved Commander. Opposition. Jealousy. Resentment. Hatred. Cruel abuse. A cross of agony and shame. But the Son of God came. He came alone. Because He loved.

Put Right With God

Years ago slavery flourished in West Africa. The slave traders rounded up large numbers of villagers for the long trek to a port of embarkation. Rough iron collars chafed their necks as heavy chains passed from collar to collar to fasten the hapless victims together in common torment.

As the dejected victims trudged through an occasional village a headman might recognize a relative or a friend. For a price he could free the fortunate person. The iron collar would come off. His head would "come out." He was redeemed.

In this part of Africa, when they speak of Christ's redemptive work, evangelists say, "God took our heads out."

When God "takes our heads out" He does a thorough work of it.

After redeeming Gomer at the slave mart, Hosea fully forgave her and took her back. As far as he was concerned, her past mistakes were a closed chapter. Let's go back to Samaria and watch the scene.

Quickly Hosea mounts the auction platform to claim his purchase. Coarse, curious men surge forward in unbelief. They recognize Hosea because they know Gomer well. What will he do with her? They do not have long to wait.

Tenderly her husband puts his arm around her as though to shield her naked form from the rough men pressing in about him. He turns sharply to a nearby merchant.

"Bring me the best robe!" he shouts, pointing to the most expensive garment on display. "Bring it quickly!"

Gently Hosea places the garment around her quivering shoulders. "Gomer, don't be afraid. You are mine—all mine at last!" he whispers in her ear, "I love you. You have nothing to fear. Come, let us go home together."

Solicitously he helps his trembling wife down from the platform. The crowd gives way in unbelief as the couple moves slowly to the dusty road that leads homeward. Her long night of sin is ending. Together they leave the crowd behind.

Hosea takes Gomer home—she who had betrayed his love and had scorned his appeals. She who had reproached and shamed him. He takes her back. Forgiving her, he loves her despite her wretched behavior. She is his wife again!

This is the way God treats the repentant sinner. He welcomes the wanderer home. When the returning child is yet "a great way off" his Father sees him and has compassion. Placing the robe of His own righteousness about him, He forgives and justifies him. All the sins of the past are cared for and he is restored. *This is the gospel.*

Kept Right With God

Hosea's story involves more than just the auction block episode. "And I said unto her, Thou shalt abide for me many days; thou shalt not play the harlot, and thou shalt not be for another man: so I will also be for thee" (Hosea 3:3).

When John writes, "If we confess our sins, he is

faithful and just to forgive us our sins, and to cleanse us from all unrighteousness" (1 John 1:9), he means that the sinner's new experience with Jesus is to continue. The forgiven, cleansed, restored experience must be a lasting one.

The man of God expected her to make a clean break with her life of sin. Hosea does not say, "Now, Gomer, you come home with me and try to be a good girl—and do the best you can."

Clearly, unmistakably, Hosea declares, "Thou shalt not play the harlot" (Hosea 3:3). His words make no provision for an up-and-down experience. Gomer is to be an overcomer. To "abide" with Hosea—to stay with him. She commences a new life—a pure life, one of victorious living.

At home Hosea tenderly nurses her to health and strength. Under his patient instruction she finds her way to the God of Israel, back to family acceptance, back to the peace of a home that honors God.

During much of her life Gomer had found herself incapable of coping with her sin problem. Only when Hosea comes and delivers her from the vise of sin can she successfully live the life of obedience and holiness.

The gospel not only saves the sinner from the *guilt* of sin; it enables the newborn saint to gain the victory over the *power* of sin.

The good news of the gospel is not "mere words. . . . You, in your turn, followed the *example* set by us and *by the Lord;* . . . thus you have become a *model* for all believers. . . ." (1 Thess. 1:5-7, NEB). "The grace of God which is given you by Jesus Christ" (1 Cor. 1:4) makes it possible. Instead of in our own power, we "can do all things through Christ which strengtheneth . . . [us]" (Phil. 4:13).

The good news of the gospel reveals a love that obeys and serves Jesus Christ. "If ye love me, keep my commandments" (John 14:15). Jesus is our example because He has the law in His heart (see Ps. 40:8). When we invite Him into our hearts, He brings the principles of love revealed in God's law with him (see Gal. 2:20).

Such a gospel Hosea brought to Gomer. Not only did the prophet redeem her—she was to *remain* with him. "You shall *stay* with me," he said (Hosea 3:3, NKJV).

But there is more! "The plan of redemption contemplates our complete recovery from the *power* of Satan" *(The Desire of Ages,* p. 311, emphasis supplied). There is a glorious "much moreness" in God's redemption plan. "The gospel according to Hosea" provides a fleeting glimpse into it.

Hosea declares, "I will betroth thee unto me for ever" (Hosea 2:19). As the words of a popular song observe, "Forever is a long, long time." God's plan includes saving us from the *guilt* of sin, the *power* of sin, and someday from the *presence* of sin. "The very essence of the gospel is restoration" *(ibid.,* p. 824).

Victory at Last!

In early March 1966 Dollis and I boarded a plane in Salisbury, Rhodesia, for Nairobi, Kenya. After eight years in the Trans-Africa Division, we were headed home on furlough. For several days we met appointments in Kenya and Uganda. On March 18 we went aboard an El Al Israel jumbo jet that would take us to Tel Aviv, Israel.

A direct flight from Nairobi to Tel Aviv would require only a few hours under normal conditions. But normal conditions do not exist in the Middle East of our day. An Israeli plane could not head directly from Kenya to Israel. They were forbidden to cross over Arab countries. Our craft had to fly over the Indian Ocean, avoiding the coasts of Yemen and Saudi Arabia. Heading up the Persian Gulf, it had to avoid penetrating the air space of any Arab states en route. The long, devious route took us to Tehran, Iran, where we made our first stop. Continuing, we passed over the mountains of Turkey, out over the Mediterranean Sea, skirting the coast of Lebanon, finally landing safely in Tel Aviv. We traveled many hundreds of extra miles to reach our destination.

It was a long, needlessly circuitous journey.

God's People Take a Detour

God's chosen people have made a long detour on the journey to their eternal homeland, too! "It was not the will of God that the coming of Christ should be so long delayed, and His people should remain so many years in this world of sin and sorrow" (*Spirit of Prophecy*, vol. 4, p. 292).

Following God's assurance in Eden (Gen. 3:15) another promise came to the people of God. "And Enoch also, the seventh from Adam, prophesied of these, saying, Behold, the Lord cometh with ten thousands of his saints" (Jude 14). Then came the day when the Lord made a special promise to Abraham. "I will make of thee a great nation, and I will bless thee, and make thy name great; and thou shalt be a blessing" (Gen. 12:2).

It was a high honor to which God called Abraham, that of being the father of the people who for centuries guarded and preserved His word to humanity.

In Moses' day the promise of special blessing came again. "And it shall come to pass, if thou shalt hearken diligently unto the voice of the Lord thy God, to observe and to do all his commandments which I command thee this day, that the Lord thy God will set thee on high above all nations of the earth" (Deut. 28:1).

"As the numbers of Israel increased, they were to enlarge their borders, until their kingdom should embrace the world" (*Christ's Object Lessons*, p. 290).

Note well that the Lord specified conditions for the fulfillment of the promise of a "chosen people": "If thou shalt hearken diligently unto the voice of the Lord thy God, to observe and to do all his commandments which I command thee." Israel fell far short of measuring up to God's requirements.

What, then, of the promises of God to Adam, to Enoch, to Abraham, to Moses, and other mighty men of God? Have God's people lost forever their promised inheritance? Will homecoming never become the glad reality God promised? Hosea, whom Jehovah used to condemn and warn Israel, brings a message of hope — the assurance that ultimately, in His own appointed time, God will fulfill His promises. His Israel *will* inherit and inhabit the earth.

God's Assurance

The prophet Isaiah foretells the glorious day of final redemption: "And it shall come to pass in that day, that the Lord shall set his hand again the second time to recover the remnant of his people" (Isa. 11:11).

Over and over, Hosea speaks with joy of the ultimate victory of God's plan and God's people: "It shall come to pass, that in the place where it was said unto them, Ye are not my people, there it shall be said unto them, Ye are the sons of the living God" (Hosea 1:10). "I will . . . make the Valley of Achor a door of hope. . . . And in that day, says the Lord, you will call me, 'My husband,' and no longer will you call me, 'My Baal.' . . . I will betroth you to me in righteousness and in justice, in steadfast love, and in mercy. I will betroth you to me in faithfulness; and you shall know the Lord" (Hosea 2:15, 20, RSV).

In the last chapter of Hosea's book we find a plaintive appeal as God calls for Israel to return to Him. Feel the love and the pathos in these compassionate words: "O Israel, return unto the Lord thy God; for thou hast fallen by thine iniquity. Take with you words, and turn to the Lord: say unto him, Take away all iniquity, and receive us graciously. . . . I will heal their backsliding, I will love them freely: for mine anger is turned away from him" (Hosea 14:1-4).

Detours fill the history of God's people through the centuries, and more may await us between now and the day when Jesus appears in the clouds of heaven. But the promise is sure: "He that shall come will come, and will not tarry" (Heb. 10:37).

To Literal Israel?

Did the Israel of Moses' day and the Israel of Hosea's day fulfill God's requirements? Will Israel, as a nation, receive the promised blessing at the coming of Jesus? Will it be an all-Israel homecoming? What do the Scriptures say?

To the prophet Daniel, God, through Gabriel, gave a vision explaining the future of Israel as His chosen people. Daniel's prophecy showed that a time would come when Israel would no longer occupy the most-favored-people status. The nation would receive 70 weeks—490 years—as a period of probation either to repent and become the people that God expected or lose its exclusive standing. The 490-year period (a part of the longer 2300-year prophecy of Dan. 8:14) commenced with "the going forth of the commandment to restore and to build Jerusalem" (Dan. 9:25).

Both secular history and God's last-day messenger help us determine its date. "The decree of Artaxerxes went into effect in the autumn of 457 B.C." (*The Great Controversy*, p. 327).

God's Word reveals Israel's failure. The nation did not repent and return to God as a people during the days before Christ, nor did it accept Jesus as the Messiah. "He was in the world, and the world was made by him, and the world knew him not. He came unto his own, and his own received him not" (John 1:10, 11).

Hatred of the Saviour finally led certain leaders to crucify Him. "Ye men of Israel, hear these words: . . . Ye have taken, and by wicked hands have crucified and slain [Jesus]" ((Acts 2:22, 23).

Daniel's prophecy indicated that the Messiah should "be cut off." "He shall cause the sacrifice and oblation to cease" (Dan. 9:26, 27). His prophecy also foretells the year of Jesus' crucifixion—the spring of A.D. 31.

In A.D. 34, after the death of Stephen, persecution set in. The Christians "were all scattered abroad. . . . They . . . went every where preaching the word" (Acts 8:1-4). This event marked the close of the 490-year prophecy and the end of the Jewish nation's exclusive status.

"At that time, through the action of the Jewish Sanhedrin, the nation sealed its rejection of the gospel by the martyrdom of Stephen and the persecution of the followers of Christ. Then the message of salvation, no longer restricted to the chosen people, was given to the world" *(The Great Controversy,* p. 328).

What About God's Promises to Abraham and Israel?

God's covenant with Israel will be implemented despite the failure of the Jewish nation before Christ. What He could not do through literal Israel in Old Testament times He will surely do through spiritual Israel. Paul sums up this transferal of divine recognition: "If ye be Christ's, then are ye Abraham's seed, and heirs according to the promise." "Know ye therefore that they which are of faith, the same are the children of Abraham" (Gal. 3:29, 7).

Though the Jewish people did not fulfill their task, the Lord has prepared a way for all—Jew and Gentile alike—to become part of His chosen people. *The*

Living Bible sums up this wonderful transaction in these words of Paul: "For God's secret plan, now at last made known, is Christ himself" (Col. 2:2, TLB).

"Though the people of Israel 'according to the flesh' had failed of the high destiny to which God had called them, in their unbelief had failed to become the light of the world, . . . yet God had not cast off the seed of Abraham; the glorious purposes which He had undertaken to accomplish through Israel were to be fulfilled. All who through Christ should become the children of faith were to be counted as Abraham's seed; they were inheritors of the covenant promises" *(Patriarchs and Prophets*, p. 476).

This adjustment of God's plan does not exclude the people of physical Israel. Now they are on the same footing as their Gentile neighbors. They must find salvation through Christ. "Neither is there salvation in any other: for there is none other name under heaven given among men, whereby we must be saved" (Acts 4:12).

Are There Different Roads to Heaven?

Some years ago I conducted an evangelistic crusade in Nagercoil, a city located at the extreme southern tip of India. An Indian Christian politician attended the services night after night. At the close of the meeting each evening he expressed appreciation for the way we presented Bible teachings.

After two or three weeks we covered things that were new to those not of our faith. One night as my politician friend paused to shake hands at the close of the service he said to me, "Preacher, there are many ways into the kingdom. You are on one road. I am on another. Every church has its own road, but we will all converge at the gates of pearl and all sweep into the gloryland together."

I paused a moment, smiled, gripped his hand warmly, and replied, "My friend, Jesus doesn't tell me that in His Word. He says there is only one road—one way into the kingdom—'I am the way, the truth, and the life: no man cometh unto the Father, but by me' [John 14:6]."

We must approach God through Christ, our Mediator. He is the only way. "This is the sinner's only hope. . . . There is only one channel and that is accessible to all, and through that channel a rich and abundant forgiveness awaits the penitent, contrite soul and the darkest sins are forgiven" *The SDA Bible Commentary*, Ellen G. White Comments, vol. 7, p. 913).

What a Homeland! What a Homecoming!

Would you know more of this fantastic homeland and homecoming? Close your eyes and imagine the scene. Christ's second advent is a resplendent reality. The sleeping saints awaken. "Then we which are alive and remain shall be caught up together with them in the clouds, to meet the Lord in the air: and so shall we ever be with the Lord" (1 Thess. 4:17).

Imagine ascending through space with the redeemed of all ages borne in chariots of God's glory— a numberless host of angels. "With songs of gladness [we will] ascend together to the City of God" *(The Great Controversy*, p. 645).

Picture the redeemed from all climes and of all ages in one vast throng on the sea of glass. Black. White. Brown. Yellow. Red. All kinds of people will be there. Here "Jesus brought the crowns, and with His own right hand placed them on our heads" *(Early Writings,* p. 16).

"When . . . the crown of immortal glory is placed upon the brow of the victor, many will raise their crowns in sight of the assembled universe and, pointing to their mother, say, 'She made me all I am through the grace of God. Her instruction, her prayers, have been a blessing to my eternal salvation' " *(Child Guidance,* p. 564). This will be my testimony—perhaps yours, too.

"With joy unutterable, parents see the crown, the robe, the harp, given to their children. The days of hope and fear are ended. The seeds sown with tears and prayers may have seemed to be sown in vain, but their harvest is reaped with joy at last. Their children have been redeemed" *(ibid.,* p. 569).

Afterward the vast throng of the redeemed, with Jesus in the vanguard, moves from the sea of glass to the city (see *Maranatha,* p. 305). In her vision Ellen White beheld the event. "Jesus raised His mighty, glorious arm, laid hold of the pearly gate, swung it back on its glittering hinges, and said to us, 'You have washed your robes in my blood, stood stiffly for my truth, enter in' " *(Early Writings,* p. 17).

"A voice, richer than any music that ever fell on mortal ear, will be heard saying, 'Come, ye blessed of my Father, inherit the kingdom prepared for you from the foundation of the world' " *(Counsels on Stewardship,* p. 350).

Home at last! The promises to Adam, to Enoch, to Abraham, to Moses, to Hosea—all gloriously fulfilled! You and I, with our family and friends, must be there. We must let God use us to share this anticipation with those around us so that they also may be there.

A Runaway Slave

"Quickly, Aliki, fetch me my sandals and two tunics. I'm leaving!" The agitated husband stormed into his home out of breath.

"But, Onesimus, what?"

"Don't talk, woman. I'm off to Rome," he snapped. "Put in a little food. It's a long journey."

"But—" she pressed.

"Hurry! Don't talk! I've stolen from the master. If Philemon catches me, it means death. You know the Roman law provides no protection for slaves."

"How long will you be gone?" Aliki struggled to put it all together.

"I don't know how long I'll be gone. I don't even know if I will ever see you again," he choked.

"What will happen to the children and to me?" she fought back the tears as she bundled up the tunics, the sandals, a few fruits, some olives, and a loaf of coarse bread.

"I don't know! All I know is that I must get out of here quickly. Do the best you can to care for the little ones. Kiss them for me. Now, I'm gone!"

Weeks later the runaway slave trudged, footsore and weary, into the outskirts of Rome. The boat trip he tried to forget. Now he must melt facelessly into the masses of the capital city.

When his few pieces of money were gone, Onesimus scavanged the garbade dumps for food until he could find work.

Onesimus and Paul Meet

Just how Onesimus met the apostle Paul the Scriptures do not reveal. Doubtless he had heard of the kindness and generosity of Christians from Philemon, his Christian master. In his extremity he may have sought help from believers in Rome, who were acquainted with Paul, then under house arrest in the city.

Contact with strangers on the part of a runaway slave posed grave dangers. Someone might turn him over to government officials. Then he would face the unhappy prospect of being sent back to Colossae for punishment—even death.

Whatever the true scenario, it is certain that the Holy Spirit was directing in his life. God saw in the fugitive someone whose heart would be receptive to the gospel story. In His own time and way Onesimus and Paul met. As a result, the fugitive became a Christian.

In spite of their friendship, Onesimus's past loomed ever large before both of them. Christianity does not provide an unscathed escape from an unsavory past. Onesimus, the Christian, must face the consequences of his wrongdoing. He must return to Colossae, make wrongs right with Philemon, and cast himself upon his offended master's mercy. The runaway slave could break neither the law of God nor the law of the land with impunity.

Having advised Onesimus to return home, the old apostle wrote a friendly letter to his master, appealing for compassion and mercy in dealing with his slave. Onesimus returned to Colossae with it.

Philemon, the Christian Slaveowner

We know little about Philemon's life. From the letter itself some interesting facts do emerge. He was a Christian convert of Paul's (verse 19). The apostle held him in high esteem, referring to him as "dearly beloved." The apostle considered him a "fellowlabourer" (verse 1). He was widely known and loved among his fellow Christians (verse 5). A Christian who communicated his faith to others easily (verse 6), he was a great "encourager" and helped maintain a healthy spirit among the believers (verse 7). Paul felt no hesitancy in approaching him with a sensitive request (verses 9, 10).

Sigmund Freud tells the story of an Oriental prince who had a remarkable dream. After he awoke, the potentate, like Nebuchadnezzar of old, could not remember what he had dreamed. He therefore sent for one of the court's wise men to come and explain the phenomenon.

"Alas, O king, I have bad news for you!" the wise man said after a few moments' reflection. "Your relatives will all die, and you will die."

The prince, angry at the news, had the man speedily executed. Then he sent for a second soothsayer.

"Rejoice, Your Highness!" the wise man said, "I have good news for you! You will survive all of your relatives."

Highly pleased, the prince elevated him to a high office. Both men had told the prince the same thing with different results. It does make a difference—not only *what* we say, but *how* we say it.

It is evident from his letter to Philemon that Paul knew not only what to say, but also how. His whole Epistle is a masterpiece of Christian tactfulness. He understood well how to employ words that draw—that win—rather than abrasive ones that repel and hurt.

Paul addressed his Christian friend as "Philemon, our dearly beloved" (verse 1) and thanked God for his presence in the church (verse 4). Thoughtfully, Paul mentioned Philemon's love and faith—two of his strong points (verse 5). In the following verse Paul acknowledged the Colossian's good works on behalf of the Christian cause. Then in verses 8-16 he did not command Philemon to do what he believes he should—rather, he reminisced, he explained, he reasoned, he appealed. Almost every sentence of the letter is perfumed with Christian tactfulness.

Tactfulness in Our Homes and Among Close Friends

It is easy to take family members and close friends for granted. Sometimes we are brusque and offensive with them. Perhaps we assume, "This person whom I have offended is part of my family, or one with whom I have been friendly for a long time, so I don't need to be careful what I say to him/her, or how I say it."

Oliver Wendell Holmes reminds us, however, "Don't flatter yourself that friendship authorizes you to say disagreeable things to your intimates. The nearer you come into relationship with a person, the more necessary do tact and courtesy become."

In our family circles Holmes' words should read something like this: "Don't think that because a person is a member of your family you can say disagreeable things to him/her and maintain a sweet loving atmosphere in your home." The fact is, the nearer you come into relationship with a person, the more necessary do tact and courtesy become.

"Give none offence [be tactful]," Paul counseled the Corinthian believers (1 Cor. 10:32). "Giving no offence in any thing" (2 Cor. 6:3). This is real tact.

"My brethren, prevail by love rather than by severity. When one at fault becomes conscious of his error, be careful not to destroy his self-respect. Do not seek to bruise and wound, but rather to bind up and heal" (*Testimonies*, vol. 7, p. 265).

You may have heard the story of Betty and her little brother Billy. As they were playing one day Betty suddenly commanded, "Billy, go into the house and get our sand bucket and little shovel."

At the moment Billy was not inclined to run any errands for his big sister. "I don't want to," he complained.

"But you have to do what I tell you. I'm older, and when I tell you to do something, you have to do it!"

"Well," her brother shot back, "If I *have* to, I *won't!*"

Don't most of us resist doing what we *have* to do?

Be an "Encourager"

Paul knew how to encourage those around him. In ways it is well for us to practice in our own family circles, Paul built up the morale and the enthusiasm of all with whom he associated. His Epistle to Philemon exudes encouragement. As you read the brief letter again, note carefully how his words inspire his associates with confidence. Hundreds of harried people around us are hurting. A few words of encouragement that we may speak could easily make the difference between hope and despair to them. Members of our own families need to hear such words often, too.

Our God is a God of encouragement. Through the centuries His stalwarts have strengthened His people. When the murmuring children of Israel faced the prospect of attack and death at the hands of Pharoah, "Moses said unto the people, Fear ye not, stand still, and see the salvation of the Lord, which he will shew you to day: for the Egyptians whom ye have seen to day, ye shall see them again no more for ever. The Lord shall fight for you" (Ex. 14:13, 14). His words nerved them to trust Him and move forward to face apparently impossible situations and to come forth victorious.

Our husbands, wives, sons, daughters, fathers, mothers, sisters, and brothers all have Red Sea experiences when bitter disappointment harasses them. They need our support. Let our words of hope cheer them on their way.

Our heavenly Father sought to inspire us through Isaiah's pen—"For I, the Lord your God, hold your right hand; it is I who say to you, 'Fear not, I will help you.' " "Fear not, for I am with you, be not dismayed, for I am your God; I will strengthen you, I will help you, I will uphold you with my victorious right hand" (Isa. 41:13, 10, RSV).

The blind man was old and tired, and he looked discouraged. As I passed him at the department store entrance he sat on a beat-up old chair, listlessly sweeping his fingers across the lifeless strings of an old guitar. His cup revealed that he too was suffering from the recession.

Slipping a dollar bill into his cup, I whispered, "God bless you, brother. Keep up your courage. God loves you," and hurried along.

I had gone but a few steps when I heard a shout

that startled the nearby pedestrians: "Praise the Lord!" The old man's head jerked up. His face brightened with new hope. With a boisterous verve, he broke into a spirited singing and strumming of a gospel hymn of praise. As I drove away a few minutes later he was still praising the Lord with gusto.

I don't tell this story to parade my philanthropy, for I don't usually drop dollar bills into the cups of strangers. Instead I use it to remind myself of a neglected principle of happiness in marriage. A little encouragement will brighten a whole day. A few loving words, a kindly act, will lift a heavy burden and set a sad heart singing. Children, too, carry burdens. They need encouragement.

Solomon describes encouragement in the following words: "Like apples of gold in settings of silver is a word spoken in right circumstances" (Prov. 25:11, NASB).

Those who are our own flesh and blood and whom we profess to love the most should be the objects of our special concern in warm Christian love, compassion, tactfulness, and encouragement. We do well to study these practical principles in Paul's brief letter to Philemon and, having read them thoughtfully, put them into daily practice in our home circles.

Pray and Tell

In verse 4 of his letter the old apostle enunciates a principle of prayer frequently overlooked: "I thank my God, making mention of thee always in my prayers" (Philemon 1:4). Paul was not only praying for Philemon, but he also *told* his friend what he was doing. A family member or a friend may miss the full blessing unless they know about it. "There is an abundance of encouragement in the certain knowledge that a beloved and respected friend is praying for us" *(The SDA Bible Commentary,* vol. 7, p. 379). Paul wanted Philemon to experience the inspiration of knowing that the apostle was praying for him daily.

Ellen White reminds us that we should follow the same practice in our homes and among those for whom we carry spiritual burden. "We are too indifferent in regard to one another. Too often we forget that our fellow laborers are in need of strength and cheer. Take care to assure them of your interest and sympathy. Help them by your prayers, and let them know that you do it" *(The Ministry of Healing,* pp. 492, 493).

"Praying and telling" is a twofold blessing. First it benefits the one who prays. Being in the presence of God feeds his spirit. The suppliant "may close every door to impure imaginings . . . by lifting the soul into the presence of God through sincere prayer. Those whose hearts are open to receive the support and blessing of God will walk in a holier atmosphere than that of earth and will have constant communion with heaven" *(Steps to Christ,* p. 99). And the person for whom we pray is likewise blessed by the realization that someone cares enough to spend time each day talking with the Lord about his personal welfare. To be aware that someone is praying for him makes him more susceptible to the impressions and the appeals of the Holy Spirit.

Like the apostle Paul, we should pray for our loved ones, and let them know that we do it.

Gospel Dynamite

I believe he was the first live murderer I had ever seen. Wilson stood less than 50 feet from me. A tall, well-built man, his powerful biceps rippled beneath sable black skin as he spoke animatedly with friends. His pleasant demeanor belied the hideous crime for which he had been convicted. The court had determined that he had used a baseball bat to bludgeon his supervisor to death, and had sentenced him to life in prison.

As I stood in the beautiful palm-studded lagoon that Sunday morning, I was waiting to witness Wilson's baptism. Turning to the prison official near me, I asked, "Has this man truly been converted, or is he only shamming religion to make things easier in the penitentiary?"

"Preacher," he replied, looking straight at me, "if I've ever seen a man converted, Wilson is that man. When he arrived in my institution, he was one of the worst prisoners I've ever had. He was surly and defiant— everything that was bad. Much of the time he was in solitary confinement!"

The officer paused. I pressed him further. "What brought about the change?"

"Well, it all started when Adventist young people came to the penitentiary to conduct meetings. At first Wilson would stand at a distance and listen. Little by little he edged closer, until he became part of the weekly group when the young people were preaching.

At one of the calls for commitment to Christ, Wilson came forward."

"Evidently it made a real change in his life," I ventured.

"Change?" the officer fairly exploded. "I'll say the gospel has made a change in his life. He is an entirely different person today. Now he is kind and thoughtful. I don't have a more cooperative man in my institution. If they were all like him, we would soon be able to close the prisons. He is a model inmate."

The officer and I watched Pastor Brown lead Wilson down into the water. Raising his hand, the pastor intoned, "Upon your profession of faith in the Lord Jesus Christ, I now baptize you in the name of the Father, the Son, and the Holy Ghost."

Wilson went down into the water as a converted killer and came up as a saint of God—a powerful demonstration of what the gospel does for a sinner who yields his life to Jesus.

"You know, Preacher," the officer commented, "as the result of his example and witness, several other prisoners have requested baptism. I wish you would come and see for yourself what the gospel according to Wilson has done. I'd like to have you speak to the inmates."

I went. I saw. I spoke. I praised God for the power of the gospel that still changes hearts and lives of men and women—even vicious murderers.

The Gospel Is More Than a Beautiful Story

Paul declares that the gospel is more than a story—it is a mighty miracle-working *power*. "I am not ashamed of the gospel of Christ: for it is the power of

God unto salvation to every one that believeth" (Rom. 1:16).

The saxifrage is a perennial plant with small white, yellow, purple, or pink flowers. It grows chiefly in rocky crevices and is thus sometimes called "the rockbreaker." In fact, its name comes from two latin words: *saxum,* "a rock," and *frangere,* "to break." I am told that the saxifrage plant appears among ruins in Palestine, where it has literally broken down buildings constructed of stone.

The gospel of Jesus Christ is also a "rockbreaker." The transformation of Wilson's life demonstrates its power. The very word—*power*—that Paul uses comes from the Greek word *dunamis,* which construes "special power." Our English word "dynamite" derives from *dunamis.*

The power of the gospel also shattered Onesimus. Besides violating God's law, he, by stealing from Philemon and absconding as his slave, broke both Greek and Roman law, thus becoming a fugitive from justice with a price on his head. Onesimus was in deep trouble with both God and the authorities of Rome. Little wonder that Paul in his letter to Philemon says that "in time past [Onesimus] was to thee unprofitable" (Philemon 1:11).

The gospel of Christ took this "unprofitable" slave and transformed him into a stalwart for Christ—one who lived up to his name—*Onesimus* means "useful." Ellen White describes the conversion of Onesimus and his character and life after his new birth: he "listened to the words of life" from Paul. He "confessed his sins, and was converted." His "piety and sincerity" endeared him to Paul *(The Acts of the Apostles,* p. 456). The slave displayed his new compassion by his tender care of the apostle.

Onesimus's conversion experience filled him with "zeal in promoting the work of the gospel," and the power of the gospel produced in him the traits "that would render him a useful helper in [Paul's] missionary labor" *(ibid.).*

The born-again child of God willingly agreed that he should return to Philemon and make things right with him. Onesimus knew better than anyone that as a runaway slave, he might forfeit his life for his decision. But he went. The gospel of Jesus Christ left him no choice.

The Gospel Changed Philemon

Most of what we know of Philemon, Onesimus's offended master, we find in the 25 verses of Paul's Epistle and in *The Acts of the Apostles*, pages 456-460.

Like the slave, the master was a converted pagan. No doubt he was all that the term implies before the gospel changed his life. The Epistle that Paul wrote to him reveals much about his change. The former pagan is now Paul's "dearly beloved, and fellowlabourer" (Philemon 1).

He became a loving Christian filled with faith in God and with confidence in his fellow saints—an admirable quality (verse 5). We find an insight into the born-again Philemon in the words: "And I pray that as you share your faith with others it will grip their lives too, as they see the wealth of good things in you that come from Christ Jesus" (verse 6, TLB).

Paul also declares, "I myself have gained much joy and comfort from your love, my brother, because your kindness has so often refreshed the hearts of God's people" (verse 7, TLB). The gospel made Philemon an ambassador of love and joy to all within his sphere of influence.

The Gospel Provides a Saviour

Paul presents the gospel in his letter to Philemon—a Christ-centered gospel. A Saviour "able also to save them to the uttermost that come unto God by him" (Heb. 7:25), He is an all-sufficient Saviour—One who saves repentant murderers, thieves, idolaters, adulterers, liars—the whole miserable lot of sinners, if they will but turn to Him. He did not "come to call the righteous, but sinners to repentance" (Matt. 9:13). In their hearts Paul, Onesimus, and Philemon all understood the truth of His words. God had rescued them from just such depths of sin.

Today we still witness the power of Christ at work in human lives. We see it in impulsive and impetuous men like Peter made patient and tolerant, immoral women like Mary Magdalene made pure, doubting souls like Thomas confirmed in faith, reprobates like Manasseh restored to righteousness, and then we recognize what Jesus can, and must, do for any of us who are sinners. No other power under heaven can thus fulfill the sinner's need.

There can be no substitute for Jesus! "Education, culture, the exercise of the will, human effort, all have their proper sphere, but here they are powerless. They may produce an outward correctness of behavior, but they cannot change the heart; they cannot purify the springs of life. There must be a power working from within, a new life from above, before men can be changed from sin to holiness. That power is Christ" (*Steps to Christ*, p. 18).

Indeed, Paul recorded a glorious truth when he

summed it all up—"Christ is all" (Col. 3:11).

He Is My Saviour and Advocate

Three times in Philemon (verses 12, 15, and 17) Paul appeals to Onesimus's master to "receive" the run-away slave and accept him back as a Christian brother. The three usages of "receive" have some interesting connotations.

In verse 12 Paul states that he is sending Onesimus to him and appeals to him, "Therefore receive him." "I am sending him back to you, sending my very heart" (RSV). What love the words convey! It was not easy for Paul to part with the slave, whom he had learned to love dearly as a Christian brother.

Later the apostle appeals again, "Receive him as myself" (verse 17). Translators of the New International Version and *The New English Bible* render it as "Welcome him as you would welcome me." Here is the measure of his hopes for a favorable reception for Onesimus. Philemon, a good friend of Paul's, no doubt would prepare a royal welcome should the man of God himself come to visit. "Welcome him [Onesimus]," Paul writes, "as you would welcome me."

What an appeal—made on behalf of a repentant sinner who at one time had been a thief, a family deserter, an ungrateful slave! If this was expecting much of Philemon, it also is a measure of Paul's affection for Onesimus.

Here Paul is saying, "Receive him unconditionally. Don't hold anything against him." Then comes his Christlike appeal: "If he has done you any wrong or is in your debt, put that down to my account. Here is my signature, Paul; I undertake to repay" (verses 18, 19, NEB).

To carry the already superlative a step higher, Paul also implies, "When Onesimus comes to your door, don't look at him. Look at me. Don't think of him as your renegade slave worthy to be punished—perhaps even by death. Think of me and what I have done for you."

It is but an imperfect illustration of what Jesus has done for sinners. But, thank God, Jesus *is* our mediator, our high priest. He appeals to His heavenly Father to welcome the penitent sinner as God would welcome Him. "Thou . . . hast loved them, as thou hast loved me" (John 17:23).

"Of course, that man—Pierson, Brown, Smith, or Jones—is a sinner," the Saviour, as my advocate, declares to the watching universe. "He doesn't deserve to be saved, but the gospel has done something for him. He has confessed his sins, has accepted My death as substitute for his. His faith is strong. Receive him."

In a sense Christ is saying, "If he hath wronged thee, . . . put that on mine account." "If he . . . oweth thee ought, . . . I will repay" (Philemon 1:18, 19). "Our dependence is not what man can do; it is what God can do for man through Christ. . . . Thank God we are not dealing with impossibilities. We may claim sanctification. We may enjoy the favor of God. *We are not to be anxious about* what Christ and God think of us, but about what God thinks of Christ, our Substitute" (E. G. White, in *General Conference Bulletin*, Apr. 23, 1901; italics supplied).

When we seek to be right with God, we need not worry about how He views us. If we come to God as penitents, Jesus accepts our guilt and stands before the Father in our stead.

There is no question regarding God's infinite love for His Son or His acceptance of the penitent who approaches Him through Jesus. "Receive him, welcome him, as You would receive Me and welcome Me," Jesus says.

Our Saviour "is able . . . to save to the uttermost" (Heb. 7:25). The Philemon letter makes this clear. Onesimus had defrauded and deserted his master, left his home and family, and broken both God's law and Roman law. He deserved punishment. On his own, he could never have made things right with Philemon. Possessing no means to make restitution, he could never have paid the debt he owed. He must have help. And help was gloriously and amply provided. This is the good news of the Philemon story.

It matters not what heinous deeds you or I may have commited. We cannot atone for our misdeeds. Alone, we are helpless before God. But, praise the Lord, we are not alone. "If any man sin, we have an advocate with the Father, Jesus Christ the righteous" (1 John 2:1). He assumes the awful debt. "Put that on my account," He says to the Father, "I will repay. Receive him."

There is yet another "receive him" in the epistle to Philemon. "Receive him *for ever*," Paul asks (verse 15). Here Paul is saying, "Philemon, receive and accept Onesimus not only now, but receive him forever. Keep him—always! Help him to be all that he ought to be. Help him to continue to live a pure, honest, upright life from now on."

I am thankful for a Saviour who not only receives me as a sinner and puts me right with heaven, but also makes me an overcomer—victorious over sin. He receives, saves, and keeps. Not only does He forgive the sins of the past, but Christ also has power to make me an overcomer victorious in Him. He can and will, if I cooperate, make it forever. "But thanks be to God, which giveth us the victory through our Lord Jesus Christ" (1 Cor. 15:57). Our yesterdays, todays, and tomorrows all are in His hands—forever. This is the precious gospel we find in Philemon, as well as the four Gospels of the New Testament.

Praise God, this gospel will do for you and me what it did for Paul, Philemon, and Onesimus.

Ye Are All One

During my study recently I ran across a new word. You may or may not recognize it, but I vow you have encountered its evil presence in today's world many times.

My new word is *ethnocentrism.*

Webster's New World Dictionary defines it as "the emotional attitude that one's own ethnic group, nation, or culture is superior to all others." Ethnocentrism insists that I and mine are better than you and yours.

Our world today is full of this philosophy of hate and division. I found it in my own beloved America as Black and White on occasion mutilated and destroyed in Washington, D.C., Chicago, Miami, and other metropolitan areas. I encountered it in Belfast as Catholics and Protestants blasted one another.

I met it in Bombay, India, as I fled from angry mobs of Hindus and Muslims battling in the street. I witnessed its devastation during the Watutsi and Bahutu tribal carnage in central Africa. I saw smoke rising from burning villages and visited refugees huddled on mission stations who had fled from tribal adversaries. I was in the midst of it in Jordan, Israel, Syria, and Lebanon as Arabs and jews existed in a cauldron of hate and suspicion.

Ethnocentrism has damned the human race since the days of Cain and Abel, Ishmael and Isaac.

Our world today is plagued with all sorts of "gaps." We have generation gaps, sexual gaps, ethnic gaps, religious gaps—gaps, it seems, of every description. But such things are not God's plan. They are the work of an enemy—*the* enemy, Satan.

The gospel of Jesus Christ is an international, interracial, interethnic message of hope, help, and unity. Paul makes it clear. "There is neither Jew nor Greek, there is neither bond nor free, there is neither male nor female: for ye are all one in Christ Jesus" (Gal. 3:28).

A Message for Us Today

Seventh-day Adventists are not nationalists—we are internationalists. Two scriptures that played important roles in making us a people emphasize this. The angel with the little scroll open in his hand, "set his right foot upon the sea, and his left foot on the earth" (Rev. 10:2). Thus John the revelator declared the Advent message of the little book to be a worldwide one destined to be proclaimed in the great metropolitan areas of earth ("the sea," heavily populated places) and in the out-of-the-way places ("the earth," sparsely populated regions).

To Everyone, Everywhere

John further writes: "And I saw another angel fly in the midst of heaven, having the everlasting gospel to preach unto them that dwell on the earth, and to every nation, and kindred, and tongue, and people" (Rev. 14:6).

The message of the little book—the everlasting gospel, the Advent message—God destines to go everywhere to everyone. It knows no caste or creed, nationality or ethnic background. God's Word declares that He loved *the world*—the *whole* world (see

John 3:16). Jesus died for everyone. In the eyes of God we are not Pakistanis, or Americans, or British, or Russians, or Tanzanians, or Indonesians, or Brazilians, or Australians, or Jamaicans. We are human beings—sinners needing to be saved.

God loves the sinner, the saint, the world's unlovable, the weak, the discouraged, the educated, the uneducated, the high, the low, the rich, the poor, the saved, the backsliders—His great heart of love encompasses us all. We are, indeed, one human race in His eyes of love and compassion.

We all love our native land. If we do not, something is radically wrong with us or with our government. I am proud to be an American. With all of its shortcomings, I still feel it is the greatest nation on earth. In 1942, when we returned home after seven years in the mission field, I stayed up most of the last night before our arrival in New York Harbor. I didn't want to miss seeing the Lady With the Torch waiting to welcome us.

But after spending many years outside my homeland, living or traveling in more than 100 countries, I have learned some valuable truths. Every land has loving and lovable people, unique and beautiful places, and stimulating challenges. My country, great as it is, doesn't have a monopoly on *all* of the physical, the historic, the cultural, or spiritual assets of earth. Christians—Seventh-day Adventist Christians—will see and appreciate the desirable, the worthy, the satisfying, and the enjoyable in every nation they visit and among every ethnic group with whom they mingle.

On occasions young missionary recruits have come to me with a familiar question: "When I go to my new field of labor, should I take and American flag with me?"

"Yes," I reply. Then, after a pause, "but be sure and keep it well out of sight when you arrive. Keep in your heart all of the treasures of your homeland, but look for all of the good things you can find in the land of your adoption."

Seventh-day Americans

I was enjoying Friday evening worship with a mission family half a world away from their homeland. When little 6-year-old Doreen prayed, she said, "Dear Jesus, please make all of the people here in India Seventh-day Americans."

At the time I smiled, but I learned an important lesson. We don't leave our homelands to make Seventh-day Americans, or Seventh-day Englishmen, or Seventh-day Frenchmen out of the people where we labor. We go to be used by the Lord to proclaim the everlasting gospel—that will make them Jesus-loving, Bible-based, faithful, overcoming, practicing Seventh-day Adventists who are useful and profitable to God, as Paul believed Onesimus would be to Philemon (see Philemon 11).

About You and Me and Diamonds

Some years ago I visited the establishment of a diamond merchant in Johannesburg, South Africa. With fascination I watched a workman shape and polish precious stones, preparing them for market. Then I noticed something that had until then escaped my untutored eye. All of the diamonds were not the same color. Some were white, some yellow, and some black.

"I notice that you have diamonds of different colors," I said as I watched the workman. "Are all the gems of equal value?"

The man at the bench smiled. "Yes," he replied. "It doesn't matter what color they are. What matters is the quality and the size of the stone."

"Is the same process used in cutting and shaping the diamonds of different colors?"

"Yes, the same process."

The experience set me thinking. It helped in solidifying my position on race relations. Adventists everywhere are busy gathering gems for God's kingdom. "They shall be mine, saith the Lord of hosts, in that day when I make up my jewels" (Mal. 3:17).

Now, all the black, white, red, brown, and yellow jewels are passing through the sometimes painful process of being cut and polished in preparation for a place in God's kingdom. Our color, our sex, our age, our ethnic or cultural background, do not matter. We all face tests and trials, discouragements, disappointments, and failures.

What should our attitude be toward jewels of another color, of a culture and national background other than our own? Paul gives us his answer in the letter to Philemon. Remember Paul's urgent appeal on behalf of a runaway slave of a different nationality and different social stratum. "Receive him. . . . Receive him. . . . Receive him." "Receive him" unconditionally. "Receive him as myself." "Receive him for ever" (Philemon 12, 17, 15).

Receive him and treat him just as you would want to be treated. "Treat men exactly as you would like them to treat you" (Luke 6:31, Phillips). "The man who makes no allowances for others will find none made for him" (Jas. 2:13, Phillips).

It would be well for all of us to be like the little boy who came running to his mother one day.

"Mama! Mama!" he cried, out of breath. "Can I bring Carl home with me?"

"Is he colored?" she asked.

"I don't know, Mama. I'll run and see."

It would be a wonderful world in which to live and a wonderful church in which to serve if all of us could approach the challenge with the same guileless charm as that boy did.

The Jesus Challenge

In his letter to the Philippians Paul has further counsel for those confronted with gap problems. "Let this mind be in you, which was also in Christ Jesus" (Phil. 2:5). Dr. Phillips translates the passage as "Let your attitude to life be that of Christ Jesus himself."

"Study carefully the divine-human character, and constantly inquire, 'What would Jesus do were He in my place?' This should be the measurement of our duty" (*The Ministry of Healing*, p. 491). It is good advice for us to follow in the home, in the place of business, in the church—in fact, in any place, at any time.

Those little postscripts on Paul's letters often contain some useful information or helpful philosophy. "Please keep a guest room ready for me," he says, "for I am hoping that God will answer your prayers and let me come to you soon" (Philemon 22, TLB).

Though in prison, Paul's spirit and letters are upbeat. "Though I'm still here in prison," he is saying, "yet because of your prayers I believe I'll be with you soon. So get ready for my visit." Here is a message of faith and courage. Paul never let the evil one get him down. He was a faith-filled, courageous warrior of the cross. Not even Caesar or his prisons could rob him of faith and hope. The old apostle has left a valuable example in Christian letter writing—we are to fill our letters with courage and hope.

Even in his closing words, though he is in prison and the future appears uncertain, he sends his warm Christian regards to Epaphras, to Marcus, to Aristarchus, Demas, and Lucas. He ends with an assurance of prayers and the pronouncement of God's grace upon his friends and fellow missionaries.

The big question, of course, is—did Paul's letter accomplish what he hoped and prayed it would?

Did Philemon receive Onesimus graciously? Did he forgive him for stealing and running away? Scripture does not answer our question. We can only speculate. But it is difficult to read Paul's brief Epistle without being deeply impressed with the old apostle's persuasiveness.

Philemon owed Paul much—"Thou owest unto me even thine own self besides" (verse 19). His moving appeals must certainly have given the man pause for careful consideration. "I . . . beseech thee." "receive him as myself." "Let me have joy of thee in the Lord." "Knowing that thou wilt also do more than I say." How could a Christian friend like Philemon resist such loving appeals so filled with confidence and expectation? Somehow I believe Paul's confidence in Philemon was justified—that he and Onesimus were reconciled.*

And What About You?

What Philemon did about Paul's loving appeal to him was of utmost importance. But what are we doing about our Saviour's appeals in our own hearts, in our own lives? Where we may be falling short of the will of God in our lives, as the Holy Spirit pleads with us to overcome sin—are we listening? More important—are we yielding? Are we letting the God of Hosea and Paul do His important work in our lives? Let us settle this most important question today!

"For he saith, I have heard thee in a time accepted, and in the day of salvation have I succoured thee: behold, now is the accepted time; behold, now is the day of salvation" (2 Cor. 6:2).

*Archaelogists have found an inscription in the ruins of ancient Laodicea. It was written by a freed slave to his former master, a man named Marcus Sestius Philemon. Could this be a clue to Onesimus's fate?